D1452755

Metaphorically a "good man" is said to be authentically a "sound tree" if, deeply rooted in faith, lifted high in hope, unfolded in love, abounding with the flowers of ardent longing, he has — like a strong, tall tree, shady and blossoming — the fruit of activity as nourishment.— St. Bonaventure, *Homilies*.

ROOTED IN FAITH

Homilies to a Contemporary World

By St. Bonaventure

Translation and Introductory Essay
by Marigwen Schumacher
Foreword by Peter Damian Fehlner O.F.M.Conv.

FRANCISCAN HERALD PRESS

1434 WEST 51st STREET ● CHICAGO, 60609

Rooted in Faith: Homilies to a Contemporary World, by St. Bonaventure. Translation and Introductory Essay by Marigwen Schumacher. Foreword by Peter Damian Fehlner O.F.M.Conv. Copyright ©1974 by Franciscan Herald Press, 1434 West 51st Street, Chicago, Illinois 60609.

Library of Congress Cataloging in Publication Data:
Bonaventura, Saint, Cardinal, 1221-1274.
    Rooted in faith.

    CONTENTS: Thanking God (1 Cor. 1:4)—Prayer (Lk. 19:46) [etc.]—Selected bibliography (p. 133).
    1. Catholic Church—Sermons. 2. Sermons, Latin—Translations into English. 3. Sermons, English—Translations from Latin. I. Title. BX1756.B58S413 252'.02   73-19533   ISBN 0-8199-0465-1

Nihil Obstat:
    Mark P. Hegener O.F.M.
    Censor Deputatus

Imprimatur:
    Msgr. Richard A. Rosemeyer, J.C.D.
    Vicar General, Archdiocese of Chicago

October 4, 1973

Commemorating
the Seven-hundredth Anniversary
of the Death of
Saint Bonaventure,
this Book Is Dedicated
with Much Love
and Deep Gratitude
to
Peter Damian Fehlner O.F.M.Conv.

Acknowledgements

The first word of acknowledgment must go to Peter Damian Fehlner O.F.M.Conv. who is, indeed, "magister mihi" in Bonaventurian studies. His deep wisdom, knowledge, and spirituality have aided my understanding and constantly encouraged my efforts.

A special word of appreciation belongs to Romano S. Almagno O.F.M. He first "introduced me" to Bonaventure and has continued to share with me his enthusiasm, expertise, and Franciscan compassion. Also to Mike Meilach O.F.M., editor of *The Cord*.

To Franciscan friends — especially Regis Gallo, Jim Collins, David Marszalek, and Frank Walter whose critique of sections of the manuscript has been invaluable — I am deeply grateful.

There are many other friends whose love and interest has continually strengthened me in this project: their names are forever written in my heart.

Contents

Illustrations

Foreword

Fashions in preaching are notoriously unstable. In an age that places great emphasis on contemporaneity considerable courage is needed to edit, as relevant to our times, sermons over seven centuries old. Nonetheless, the seventh centenary of the death of St. Bonaventure, Bishop and Doctor of the Church, is a providential opportunity for underscoring not only his abiding significance for the Church and Christians, but to make available for the first time in English a representative sample of a long neglected part of his works, namely, his sermons.

Though every generation fancies no other has ever endured a crisis like its own, in fact the current unrest and confusion in the Church is hardly as original as we imagine it to be. As we draw nearer to the final day of history, the day of the glorious and final coming of Christ the Lord, the onslaughts of the prince of this world grow stronger, perhaps, in intensity against the followers of the Lamb. But the nature of those onslaughts, the defences available against them, and the final outcome for the Church and for every Christian determined to remain with Christ, the true vine, are what they have been from the day of Christ's exaltation on the cross and will continue to be until the day of judgment.

Every saint and doctor of the Church enjoys a contemporaneity with every other generation of Christians, because in his life and in his thought he is a witness or martyr to the truth that Jesus is the Christ, the Son of the living God, and that there is a providential purpose in history and in the life of every human person made manifest in the work of salvation and in the judgment of God on infidelity and evil. St. Bonaventure is no exception to this rule;

indeed, he is a unique example of its validity and fruitfulness. In a manner rarely encountered even in other saints and doctors, he combines the qualities of teacher of minds and hearts, pastor of souls, and mystic lover of Christ and the Church. Nowhere is this so evident as in his sermons where he is at once concerned with effective, practical instruction that will guide and draw the flock entrusted to his care into those verdant pastures where they might feast on the food of heaven, enjoy the love of the Savior.

That Bonaventure should be so little known in the English-speaking Catholic world is not evidence of his lack of impact on the life of the Church over the centuries. Even a cursory examination of his life and work would reveal innumerable and hitherto unsuspected contributions. But that one who has done so much for the Church, and who could and would do so much more, should be ignored, or, when known be misunderstood, does argue a need for sound introductions, not as a substitute for Bonaventure, but to help us overcome the obstacles blocking our perception of the limpid thought, profound insight, and delightful art of a master in Israel.

Most of the initial frustration encountered in a first study of Bonaventure can be reduced to three categories: intellectual, artistic, and linguistic. The homiletic corpus of any preacher involves problems, common enough through the centuries, which Marigwen Schumacher succintly analyzes in her introduction.

A not infrequent impression of Bonaventure, met among scholars, is that of a man of great learning, brilliant intellect, but narrow and superficial understanding; one who today might be called a pietist or fundamentalist, the militant conservative bending his every energy to buttress, with irresistible logic, the traditional and official views of his Church, hostile to all innovation and fearful of scientific progress.

There is no doubt that Bonaventure rates wisdom above science of any kind, that, for him, learning is an exercise, a discipline for the sake of understanding and contemplation, that we might be good, and chiefly the latter. And surely he insists on the prior acceptance of the Truth, of a total synthesis centered on Christ and mediated by His Church, before the application of any methodical, logical analysis point by point, premise by premise, of the individual propositions of the synthesis. All stand or fall together on the basis of what he calls Christian wisdom with St. Paul, and, elsewhere with St. Augustine, metaphysical exemplarism.

So, in the end, tradition does take precedence over arbitrary innovation and piety over knowledge and technique, not to their exclusion in favor of mere religious sentiment or emotion, but to their conversion into what they ought to be: sacred not secular; holy, not profane; not used for worldly gain, but leading to union with Christ and His Church whose apex, in this life, is that wonderful and singular sacrificial banquet called the Eucharist.

It is not at all arbitrary or unreasonable, emotional and irrational, that the proper cultivation of the intellect should begin and end with a total act of faith in the person of Christ and confidence in His work. The reason for this is, essentially, very simple to grasp. The existence of the person centers on the love and enjoyment of the good for its own sake, the condition for which is an unconditional assent to the truth. Faith is that first gift of God that reverses self-centeredness and lifts the mind and heart to obey the truth fully, the plain vision of which is the connatural term of a life of faith. In a word, it is the nature of conscience to include a sign of the existence of Truth which is God; otherwise neither intellect, nor thought, nor conscience would exist.

Such a starting point, however, does lead to a unique and radically different style of reflecting, that of the *fides quaerens intellectum*, one which challenges not only our piety, but also our intellect, not only the intellectual fashion of the thirteenth century, but those of every age, especially our own. Human science, secular learning and technology, where divorced from that wisdom and light that is Christ, never transcend the level of opinion, and ultimately fall into the darkness of error. Wisdom on the other hand is certain, is rooted in the eternal art and the truth that is Jesus Christ, and is thus the basis of that peace and serenity of mind that opinion cannot provide and which only Christ can give.

The logic of Bonaventure's position is rooted in the desire for truth at the heart of all personal existence, a desire that cannot find fulfillment either in the things of creation or in the human mind. Things in themselves, the objects of science, considered by themselves are known as changeable and changing, thus unreal and untrue. Their reality is only grasped when understood in the Truth of which they are the shadow and vestige, by which they have been drawn from the nothingness of unreality and for whose glory they are preserved from ending in nothing. Nor is the human mind, the reflecting subject, by itself any better source of that peace to which it is ordered. For human thought and art, practiced apart from Him in whose image Adam was made, attains a value not exceeding the fictitious and only achieves truth and beauty when freely related to that fontal light that is the Eternal Word from whom and through whom and for whom every good comes. And where created objects take the place of God as good and pleasurable in themselves, or worse, where merely human thought and opinion or utility answers the need for certainty and peace, there we find the root of that atheism, that infidelity to the truth and idolatry, whose counterpart in the moral order is selfish love, whose expression is a lifestyle centered on personal pleasure not scrupling to abuse Creator and creation alike, and whose end is despair and self-destruction.

Bonaventure's whole effort as teacher is pastoral: to bring men to love the true Light, and all whom He enlightens; to love Him who alone is Truth and the font of all that is true in things and in men, the one Master of all. To love this Light, of nature, of the law, and of grace, postulates on our part an act of faith whose object he calls "fontal," and which is the Word eternal. Can this Word be found and known for whom He is? Yes, for the Word became flesh and dwelt among us. The Incarnation is the work of grace. It need not have been, but now that He has been born of the Virgin and given His flesh for the life of the world, there is no reason not to live in the light of truth and give thanks for the wonderful works of God. To help bring the Incarnate Word into our minds and hearts as the inspired word is the goal of Bonaventure's Christian philosophy.

In an age that takes for granted the omniscience of science and the omnipotence of technology, and so assumes unlimited licence to think and do as it pleases in all things irrespective of God's law, such views cannot but appear as out-moded relics of a credulous generation. Question the assumptions behind the idolizations of science, technology, and human freedom, and affirm that understanding and assent to the truth or wisdom is not co-terminal with science, that academic and scientific freedom are not absolute and unlimited, that all secular progress is not always for the best, that all experience called "love" is not good and unselfish, that faith is much more than an element of the person's emotional life: then the relevance of Bonaventure's Christian metaphysics of the cross becomes a live issue. Even a cursory study of such masterpieces as the *Conferences on the Hexaemeron*, the *Disputed Questions on the Trinity*, and *on the Knowledge of Christ*, the *Breviloquium* and *Itinerarium* reveals that the characteristic scientific, secular bias of the thirteenth century was identical with ours, that the specific errors and intellectual perils to faith from which Bonaventure called back the wandering sheep are the same, and that Bonaventure has discerned and addressed himself to the most radical questions a faith seeking understanding and a heart seeking peace might raise in any age.

Linguistically and artistically the writings of Bonaventure, over the course of time, have become further and further removed from the reader without specialized preparation. Until the appearance of Jose' de Vinck's translations, only a few of these writings were translated into English, and then often in a style hardly adequate to the artistic merit of the original. Only a small proportion of the secondary literature on Bonaventure is in English, and this little often written for and available only to the specialist. Bonaventure himself employs a style calculated to express the reflection of the divine in this world, especially the world of grace, a reflection that is triune and made plain to us in the mystery of the Incarnation and of the Church. *Prima facie* his art can easily strike one as artificial and mechanical, a pedagogical device for inculcating key dogmas of the Church. While our problems in appreciating Bonaventure's intellectual synthesis may stem from our own bias rather than any inherent weakness of his theology, there is surely more objective ground for complaint if the well-disposed reader fails to find in the words of Bonaventure the understanding and experience, depth of knowledge and intensity of love alleged to pervade the writings of the Saint.

To my knowledge, Marigwen Schumacher is the first English translator of the Seraphic Doctor to give special attention to problems of language and style, as well as of content, and to try to find English form for Bonaventure's thought that will capture to some recognizable degree the spirit of his Latin style, the exquisite choice of words, rich in classical as well as current associations, the competent and sensitive mastery of the *cursus*, the delicate balance of thought and rhythm, the tasteful use of triadic divisions to explain a world whose nature it is to reflect and give glory to the triune God. And if we hold, with Augustine and Bonaventure, that beauty is but truth as it manifests an order, a harmonious proportion between the one and the many, then where the Truth that is God, one and three, is well expressed, the style of Bonaventure will be found to be one connaturally ordered to help in realizing that visual and auditory form of the truth, that music and art revealing the supreme loveliness and loveableness of the Word Incarnate, the King of ages.

Bonaventure would be the last to have us think him the original source of his wisdom. First and last he always thought of himself as the faithful steward of the deposit of faith given by his Master, Christ, and handed on by the Apostles, and then to those of his servants to whom he was most deeply indebted for the grace of Christian wisdom and instruction, Augustine, Gregory, Anselm, Bernard, Hugh, and Alexander of Hales. This humility by no means reduced him to the status of a slavish imitator of his instructors, but is the cause of his inner strength of character, beauty, and originality of thought. The deeply personal character of his thought, the power of his mind and the modesty and charity of its expression may, in part, be the direct effect of the influence which St. Francis of Assisi exercised on Bonaventure. The content and style of Bonaventure's works are but aspects of a single, all-embracing form of life wherein the intellect as well as the will and affections are sanctified, and whose name is Christian poverty, the following and imitation of the crucified Savior. It was through Francis, herald of the great King, that John Fidanza, later known as Bonaventure, a 25-year-old student in the Faculty of Arts of the University of Paris, who at one point had considered following his father's footsteps in the medical profession, was brought to Christ, to consider and then follow a religious and priestly call. The rest of his life was spent in the care and cure of souls, a service whose manifold dimensions are reflected in the selection of sermons contained in this volume.

While no translation can ever hope to equal the original, the explanations and notes of Marigwen Schumacher, the representative selection and careful rendition into English, should help a wider public better to appreciate someone whose appeal is perennial, and to create a desire to enjoy his company more. The translator deserves the thanks of all admirers of Bonaventure for her courage in undertaking this work and for bringing it to so successful a conclusion.

St. Anthony-on-Hudson
Rensselaer, N.Y.
June 13, 1973   Fr. Peter D. Fehlner, OFM Conv.

The original handwriting of St. Bonaventure. Copy of folio 39v of manuscript in the Public Library of Assisi, microfilmed for the College of St. Bonaventure at Quaracchi (near Florence) — now at Grottaferrata (near Rome). An enlarged xerox-copy is in the Friedsam Memorial Library, St. Bonaventure University, St. Bonaventure, N. Y.

Introductory Essay

∞∞∞∞∞∞∞∞∞∞∞∞∞∞∞∞∞∞∞∞∞∞∞∞∞∞∞∞∞∞∞∞∞∞∞

Bonaventure (1217 - 1974) was born at Bagnorea—between Viterbo and Orvieto—in Italy in 1217 [1] and died in 1274 at Lyons. His 57 years were filled with activity in intellectual-spiritual realms and in the spheres of practical administration. After his early training and entry into the Order of Friars Minor at Paris, he studied at the University under great Masters such as Alexander of Hales. Then he, too, became a "university professor" lecturing in philosophy and theology at the School of the Friars Minor in Paris and eventually, after disputes[2] between institutions were resolved, also was accorded the position of Regent Master at the University of Paris.

At the age of 40, while still teaching at Paris, he was chosen minister-general of the Order of Friars Minor. He held this office for 17 critical years as the Order continued to expand rapidly and demandingly. While minister-general, Bonaventure continued, at times, to lecture at Paris[3] but also spent much time travelling to visit the various houses of the Friars in France, Italy, Spain, and Germany. To him fell the responsibility to plan and conduct the Pentecost chapter meetings of the Friars and much of the administrative work of the Order.

He was friend and advisor to kings and popes, counselor to individuals and religious communities.[4] He managed to refuse the appointment as archbishop of York in 1265 by persuading Pope Clement IV that his duties to the Friars needed his full attention. In 1273, however, Pope Gregory X insisted unyielding that he accept the post of cardinal and that of bishop of Albano—even if this meant relinquishing his position of minister-general of the Friars. Bonaventure's last year was mostly spent in the double task of working

with the pope to prepare and then to conduct the second
Council of Lyons and the equally demanding preparations
for a general chapter to elect his successor as minister-
general. He died unexpectedly on July 15th, 1274, while the
Council was still in session at Lyons.

During this busy life of professorial and ministerial duties,
Bonaventure wrote a number of scholarly philosophical dis-
sertations and theological treatises. The range and breadth
of these is staggering: his intellectual genius and synthesis
of knowledge and spirituality is awesome in its simplicity
and beauty. A mere listing of his writings indicates their
scope and range; their chronological order attests to his
constant involvement with writing amidst all his other
duties.[5] It is not possible to discuss all of them here; and
to single out one or two for comment would be unfair to
the others. In addition to these, from his first years as a
teacher at Paris right up until his death[6] at Lyons, Bonaventure preached frequently—one might almost say constantly. His homilies were delivered in the great new Gothic
cathedrals of Europe as well as in humble parish churches.
He preached before the king and queen in the royal chapel,
before the faculty and students of the university, the schools
of the Friars, of the Dominicans, and to congregations and
groups of "ordinary folk" in various towns.[7]

Just as his homilies chronologically parallel his active pro-
fessional years, so they also, in theme and content, parallel
his lengthier philosophical and theological discourses and
his Franciscan tracts. They are, therefore, another avenue
into his thought, his insight, his synthesis. They pose no
contradiction nor deviation from his more "in-depth" writings
and lectures. It is the same man who argues the detailed
Disputed Questions on the Holy Trinity and who preaches
the homily *on the Trinity,* or writes the *Vitis Mystica* and
preaches on Easter Monday on the text "my flesh has
bloomed again." The same deep Christian faith and love are
there expressed. But the Homilies are briefer, complete in
themselves rather than one of a series of lectures, and
intended usually for delivery within the Eucharistic Liturgy.[8] Hence their teaching is more direct, their imagery

more vivid, their stylistic expression more mellifluous and powerful. Bonaventure himself was very conscious of the role and responsibility of the preacher—and also of his personal responsibility in the training of future Franciscan preachers. It is illuminating to reflect upon some of his own statements as found in introductory paragraphs of his homilies and also in his "Franciscan" writings. Perhaps, first, however, it is necessary to consider the traditions of preaching and the milieu of the twelfth and thirteenth centuries for it is only in this context that the innovative response of Francis—and consequently of his followers and inheritors in the Order of Friars Minor—can be evaluated.

Throughout the Patristic Age and the early Christian Middle Ages, preaching was the function of the bishop[9] — the *pastor* caring for his flock, instructing them in the faith and inspiring them towards perfection. Life was fairly simple, mostly rural, and God-fearing. But as we move into the twelfth century[10] —the early or "first" Renaissance—the world is changing rapidly and radically. The impact of the Crusades, not only in matters of religion but also in opening new routes of trade and commerce and re-awakening artistic and intellectual contacts with the Byzantine and Arabic worlds, stirred new beginnings. The rise of the universities at Paris, Oxford, Boulogne, and elsewhere, jostled regional insularities, mandated new life-styles, and created a ferment for thinking, feeling, experiencing, questioning. The movements of peoples and goods—static in the preceding centuries—became again a fact of life. Creativity blossomed in art, music, architecture; in literature, poetry, philosophy. The traditional subjects of the Trivium and Quadrivium were stretched to explore new ideas and include new knowledge. The secular world—now increasingly an urban civilization—bustled with activity and prosperity. Burgeoning technology created an enthusiasm for material possessions. At the same time, rampant heresies posed severe threats to Christian beliefs. Bishops were now no longer able to be the sole instructors and preachers for their people; many of the parish priests did not have enough education to meet the needs of increasingly well-educated and widely travelled parishioners in the complexity of contemporary life. Formal "religion" is always uneasy when thinking minds are questioning; but faith, when it appears most shaken, is often really being "pruned to bear greater fruit." In these somewhat chaotic conditions arose the Mendicant Orders—the Dominicans or Order of Preachers and the Franciscans or Order of Friars Minor. Two innovations were important: the members of these Orders were not geographically static as in the monastic communities and their primary function was to preach as they travelled ceaselessly about the countryside. Both Orders were involved in litigation and with opposition from within the structured Church but papal decrees and privileges gradually won them recognition and acceptance. [11]

Francis, well-known for his own simple, effective, spontaneous preaching to birds, animals, and people, emphasizes the importance of preaching—and the need for competence in it—both in the First Rule, chapter 17, and again in the Revised Rule, chapter 9. And Bonaventure, in his *Explanation of the Rule*, clarifies and amplifies, e.g., "No friar ought to preach unless he knows how to express and organize his words effectively." He concludes his remarks on chapter 9 of the Rule in this way:

"From this chapter it is obvious that Friars have a mandate to study in accordance with the intention of B. Francis since they cannot analyze and express teachings in the needed manner without study. It is also obvious that Friars from their profession have a responsibility of preaching since their Rule emphasizes it in a special section on the duties of the preacher. [12]

Again and again in the opening sections of his homilies, as he gathers the minds and hearts of the congregation together prayerfully to hear the word of God, Bonaventure speaks about preaching. He says, for example, that there are three qualities that "ought to be part of the duty of preaching: (1) holiness of service, (2) truth of faith, and (3) authority of office."[13] "It is important," he says elsewhere, "to measure out prudently the divine word according to the capacity of those listening in order not to speak

too fully nor too briefly, too eruditely nor too colloquial-
ly."[14]

We can be certain that Bonaventure—saying such things
to others—practiced and lived them himself. Not only do
the texts of his homilies reinforce his words but we also
have preserved in early Franciscan chronicles and papal
bulls statements which witness to the powerful effects of
his preaching. Blessed Francis of Fabriano, for example,
a younger contemporary of Bonaventure, observed that Bonaventure "was a holy, just, and reliable man, God-fearing,
accredited in arts at the University of Paris. . . . He was
most eloquent, possessed an outstanding knowledge of Sacred Scripture and of theology. Moreover, he was a beautiful homilist to the clerics and preacher to the people. When
he spoke, wherever he was, every tongue grew silent."[15]

Sixtus V, in his Bull, *Triumphantis Ierusalem*, of March
14, 1588, states, in part: "There was in St. Bonaventure
that unusual and special gift: he had an outstanding perception in discussion, a fluency in teaching, a keenness in
explaining. In addition he had that rare power of arousing
hearts and minds. . . [16]

But what type of homily did Bonaventure preach? What
was expected and needed in those days, in that milieu?
Fortunately there have been preserved, in various manuscripts from the twelfth to the fifteenth centuries, numerous texts of homilies—some *in toto*, some in more mutilated
form—preached by Bernard, Anthony, Thomas, Bonaventure,
and others. There are also large numbers of "Handbooks
on Preaching," on the "Techniques of Homiletics"—the
Artes Praedicandi. Although most of these are anonymous
or falsely attributed—there is, for example, both a "Pseudo-
Bonaventure" and a "Pseudo-Thomas" *Ars Praedicandi*—
some are legitimate works of well-known figures such as
Alan de Lille (c. 1128-1202) whose *Summa de arte praedicatoria*[17] was among the first treatises of this kind. Both
texts and handbooks agree in structure and form: the one
creating or following the precepts and instructions set forth
in the others. As is to be expected, the greater number of
these "handbooks" stem from the fourteenth and fifteenth

centuries—after the era of the greatest preachers. For here, as in other areas, the "rules" are formulated to teach lesser minds what the genius of an inspired preacher has already done. Nevertheless it is significant that Alan de Lille wrote his treatise near the beginning of this period and, without doubt, his influence affected his contemporaries and later preachers as well as subsequent formulations in manuals and textbooks. The form outlined in these manuals—and followed in most of the homilies—may seem to us today too elaborate, contrived, somewhat artificial, and overly-structured—and they could be so. But our critique must always keep in mind the milieu out of which these techniques grew.

The rhetoric developed in the political arenas of the Graeco-Roman world continued as a force in education[18] in the later Roman Empire long after its function in politics had been effectively silenced. The *Declamationes* and *Suasoriae* preserved for us by Seneca the Elder[19] provide us with insight into the techniques employed even when the subject-matter moved into the unreal and mythical realms so distant from the intensely practical involvement of Cicero.

And the Church inherited these traditions through her converts—men like Augustine, Jerome, Ambrose, and others. Men well-trained in the pagan schools of rhetoric now turned these techniques and skills to the service of the Faith. And the mediaeval scriptoria maintained and fostered them. The phoenix of Graeco-Roman education rose again in the schools established by Charlemagne. The Trivium—Grammar, Rhetoric, Dialectic—followed by the Quadrivium—Arithmetic, Music, Geometry, Astronomy—the "seven Liberal Arts"—knew new vitality. But the oratory of the Christian Age was sacred not political. The preacher was the inheritor and the utilizer of the gifts and techniques of persuasion and teaching. Thus it is that the *Artes Praedicandi* become, in many ways, the direct successor of Quintilian's *De Institutione Oratoria*. The rhetorical dictum of "to persuade, to teach, to delight" enjoys renewed life in the context of Sacred Scripture and divine inspiration.

But, as in Rome so in Paris, political oratory or homilizing is a combination of mind and emotion—of word and gesture—of thought and voice. Unfortunately our manuscripts record only the evidence of mind, word, thought. Thus their analysis seems dry, verbose, and heavy; it lacks the life and breath of feeling, the emphasis of gesture and resonant voice. It has been said that oratory is the most fragile of all forms of communication for it is "the energizing of a message by a speaker for a specific audience."[20] The difficulty, therefore, of its tranmission is fundamental. Even today, despite technological advances such as television, tape-recorders, satellites, cameras, and on-the-spot-reporters, it is still not possible to truly recreate the atmosphere— often charged with emotional tensions and packed with the vibrations of human bodies. Nor can the media transfer to us the reflex action of these upon the speaker (or his on them for it is a mutual response)—be he a political candidate or a preacher of the Lord. We must then, when we read these homilies, try to *hear* them; when we analyze the manuals, attempt to *see* them in their totality of performance. In other words, it is up to us to breathe life into them, recreate them from and through our own experiences of such events—transfering our tempo and timing to their historic moment.

One other point must be kept in mind as we consider these "Techniques of Homiletics," the *Artes Praedicandi*. They were written—at least the ones whose authors we know—in a university milieu, Paris and Oxford especially. They were written by preachers who, like Bonaventure, were Masters at the University and officially delegated with the responsibility and the privilege of preaching regularly to the faculty and students of the institution. These were intelligent men who understood that the kinds of questioning and formulating that were standard in the lecture halls of philosophy were also to be employed in the pulpits of theology. They realized that minds trained to logical disputation in secular subjects could not be touched by sloppily-expressed, sentimental platitudes but, rather, that vigorous expression and rigorous logic must be united in their preaching as they propounded the Sacred Scriptures.

The sections of a homily as set forth in these various

handbooks[21] are: (1) Theme, (2) Subtheme, (3) Division, (4) Confirmation, (5) Distinctions, and (6) Expansion. The *theme*, upon which the whole discourse is structured, was chosen from Scripture. At this time, however, before the standardization of liturgy under Pius V, there were often local variations in lectionaries and the preacher had great freedom in his choice of theme-text. Bonaventure usually chose his theme from the Gospels or Epistles but, frequently, uses Old Testament texts as his source. In contrast to—or in reaction against—the pastoral homilies of the earlier ages which had been more concerned with the whole Gospel passage read that day, medieval preaching chose one verse or phrase of Scripture and developed it thematically by drawing together other Scripture texts that reinforced, expanded, and "fleshed out" the chosen theme. The *subtheme*, or *pre-theme*, used another Scripture text as a basis for introductory statements focusing upon the present moment and gathering those present into prayer prior to the actual preaching. Although there was no necessary connection between theme and subtheme, obviously a subtle relationship between them could deepen the unity and impact of the preacher's message. The subtheme frequently closed with an invitation to prayer for divine inspiration— for both preacher and congregation.[22] After this prayer, the theme was always restated. This marked the beginning of the formal preaching and accommodated those perennial latecomers[23] who had not heard the first statement of the chosen text. The *division* of the theme stated the three —usually, a Trinitarian emphasis—points to be developed in the homily; the *confirmation* restated these points with the section of the Scriptural theme to which each related. The *distinctions* were simply sub-divisions of the various major divisions.

To clarify these terms, consider the following brief outline preserved of one of Bonaventure's homilies for the feast of the Asecnsion.[24] The manuscript identifies it as "a homily of Friar Bonaventure to the Friars in Chapter at Paris."

[Theme] "The one who descended is the same one who

rose higher than all the heavens to fill all things (Eph 4:10)."

[Division] "We are able to consider here three points: (1) the beckoning guidance of the one who is ascending, (2) the glorious condition of his ascension, and (3) the fruitful result of his ascension."

[Confirmation] "The first is indicated in the words "the one who descended"; the second, by "is the same one who rose higher than all the heavens"; and the third, by the words "to fill all things.""

[Distinctions] "Reflect, on the whole text, that one who wishes to ascend into the heavens with Christ ought first of all, following the example of Christ, to descend in two ways: (1) through re-learning his own sinfulness, and (2) through re-seeing his own weakness. Such a person ascends in two ways: (1) to contemplate the extent of divine majesty, and (2) to implore the pouring forth of divine mercy "to fill all things" interiorly with his gift of wisdom and fullness of grace. Since the Apostles were men of this type, they were filled with the Holy Spirit on the day of Pentecost."

That is all that has been preserved of this particular homily. In its actual delivery, however, each of the divisions and sub-divisions would be developed. *Expansion* involved a combination of proof of the various points stated in the division and an elaboration of the theme through support from other Scripture and patristic sources, from argumentation, from a weaving of imagery and inspiration to capture the imagination and emotional response in assent to the impact of the intellectual message presented. Obviously, the expansion of the chosen theme occupied the greatest proportion of time— and demanded the greatest ingenuity from the preacher especially when he was using very familiar texts on very basic feasts. Obviously, too, the manuals spent most of their chapters on various methods, i.e., "keys," of expansion.

The *Ars Concionandi*, [25] long attributed to Bonaventure but now generally regarded as "pseudo-Bonaventure"—and yet even this false attribution tells us something—lists eight types of expansion:

1. Definition, interpretation; 2. Division; 3. Reasoning, syllogizing, giving examples, etc.; 4. Agreement of authori-

ties, i.e., Scriptural and Patristic; 5. Similar word-meanings, nuances, etc. 6. Expansion of metaphors; 7. Expansion of theme: (a) literal, (b) allegorical, (c) tropological, (d) anagogical; 8. Cause and effect.

Some manuals are even more elaborate and detailed in their listings of expansions explained through numerous examples.

Such "Rule-Books" reflect the *status quo* particularly in the academic atmosphere. There is also, however, an awareness of the responsibility of the preacher to adapt his method to the needs of the people who are being instructed. For example, the *Ars Concionandi* recommends that the "division follow a pattern of either *intra* or *extra* depending on the needs of the congregation." The division "extra" is especially recommended for use "with the people." In this plan, the theme is explained through texts and images "outside" the theme-text being preached upon. The division "intra," recommended for clerics, moves "within" the theme-text and its divisions are less obvious. There is also a statement that these divisions can be helpful to the preacher "if he will make the effort to gather these under brief headings and memorize them." Lest the technique become static and mere rote, however, the *Ars Concionandi* urges individual flexibility: "without doubt there are many more divisions of this text which a skilled preacher will discover and which are better than the examples given here."

Bonaventure in his homilies, especially perhaps those given in Paris at the University, uses this expected, developing formula. The very fact that the *Ars Concionandi* was then attributed to Bonaventure reinforces the belief that he "wrote the rules" as well as followed them. He is a man of his times. But his reputation is of one who was possessor of that "unusual and special gift," "most eloquent," and who "had that rare power of arousing hearts and minds" so that "when he spoke, wherever he was, every tongue grew silent."[26] Such testimony does not accrue to one who merely slavishly follows the rules set forth in the standard treatises on "How to Give a Homily"! In order to ascertain what made Bonaventure so famed a preacher, it is impera-

tive to analyze *how* he used the precepts found in the manuals—and how he himself helped to formulate them. In what
ways is he innovative or "different"? What especially does
he do with the types of expansions? Consider the interrela-
tions of theme and subtheme, the adaptations of divisions
"intra" or "extra" according to congregation. Where and
why does he depart from the supposed rules? How, from the
written word, can we sense something of the actual delivery
of his homilies—remembering all that we must supply to
make the reading into the live experience which it originally
was. Hopefully these questions and others like them will be
answered by the selections included in this volume. I do not
wish to impose my answers upon the readers for theirs are
equally valid, whether in agreement or variance with mine.

One important dimension which is lost in reading—and
irretrievably lost in translation—is that of the sound of
words, the rhythm and cadence of sentence, the musicality
of phrase and pause which is so important and integral an
aspect of oratory, preaching, and poetry. In all of his writings—and of necessity in his speaking—Bonaventure is inheritor and practitioner of the stylistic traditions developed
by his predecessors Since Cicero's writings[27] were the
textbooks for the Trivium as they had been for the Empire,
the cadence of his sentence patterns—superbly calling forth
that which is most beautiful in the Latin language—was the
accepted norm for the medieval Schoolmen. The developments of Ciceronian *clausulae* into the Gregorian *cursus*
parallels the movement from quantitative to accentual verse
forms which came to fruition with Ambrose. The suggestion
is appealing[28] that the "Ambrosian Hymn" really just
legitimizes and accords rightful place to the natural, native
accentual rhythms of Latin found in the earliest Saturnian
verse. The destruction of the ages and the vagaries of time
have preserved for us in manuscripts only a very small frac-
tion of Classical Latin texts—and all of these are from the
aristocratic milieu! We have no texts from the "man in the
street" nor copies of the equivalent to our "Daily News."
But it is plausible (especially when one remembers that the
hexameter and stanza forms were consciously adapted from

their Greek counterparts—an example of Horace's famed dictum "Captive Greece took captive her captors") that the beat of folk dances and marching Songs persisted throughout the Roman era and emerged triumphantly in the Christian—as converts, many of them from the simple folk, brought with them all their pagan environmental assets. Ambrose, product of the pagan schools of rhetoric and yet close to his people, illustrates the merger[29] of quantitative and accentual rhythms. Compare, for example, *Aĕtērnĕ rērūm cōndĭtŏr*—considered as quantitative meter—with *Aetérne rérum cónditór*—considered as accentual verse. And the Gregorian *cursus*, developed for and by the Roman Curia, reflects this same accentual rhythm giving cadence and elegance to sentence structures written and spoken. "*Cursus* consists of ordering the elements within clauses . . . in such a way that these units end in one of three rhythmic patterns: (1) *cursus planus—vĭncla perfrégit:* (2) *cursus tardus—vĭncla perfrégerat:* or (3) *cursus velox—vĭnculum frègerámus.*"[30] These "typical fulfillments of rhythmical expectation"[31] appear regularly in the collects and prefaces of the liturgy and in the prayers of the office. Exactly how much of this is intentional rhetorical technique as opposed to the natural rhythmic essence of Latin is hard to determine. Nevertheless, both people and priest were familiar with these patterns and the psychological message they provided. As with rhythmic melody, so the rest of the panoply of rhetorical devices was adapted, elaborated (especially by Isidore), and transferred to Christian theme and Christian purpose.

Bonaventure is an expert in "vigorous expression" as well as "rigorous logic." The logic is easily seen in the subtlety of his divisions and distinctions; his prose style reflects that synthesis, in him, of rhetorical techniques, poetic rhythms, and visionary imagery which is basic to his spirituality. Because so much of this is tightly bound up with the nature and structure—and sonorousness—of the Latin language, it is out of place in an introduction to a volume of translations of his writings to speak at length of his use, for example, of assonance and alliteration, patterns of *cursus*, verbal pairings and contrasts. These simply cannot—and ultimately should not—come through in translation. Some facets of his stylistic ability can, however, be felt in translation and should be noticed. Among these are his real skill in expressing the various subtleties of each theme and the power resulting from his constant triple and quadruple divisions. And even with the help of a secretary and the availability of some sort of compendium of quotations, there is "something remarkable" in Bonaventure's ability to interweave into his preaching those pertinent Scriptural and Patristic "proofs." Moreover, there is a freshness and exactness—often a cause of enchantment as well as frustration for the translator—in his choice of words and nuances of meanings. The aptness and extraordinary quality of his use of metaphor, image, simile frequently makes concrete the intangible. His knowledge of natural phenomena, everyday crafts, and human experiences always beautifully reinforces his Trinitarian vision of God. One also feels, at times, his pungent attacks on his contemporaries and the various abuses and "happenings" of the day. In many ways, then, admiration, awe, and delight, transform us as we are challenged, even startled by the directness and depth of Bonaventure, the preacher.

Although this present edition is the first attempt to make Bonaventure's *Homilies* available in English translation, the Quaracchi edition of his *Opera Omnia* has edited some 700 of them in their Latin text; the Latin-Spanish edition also includes several, grouped within its plan.[32] More recently, additional manuscripts have been found to contain homilies which scholars agree are "genuine Bonaventure." We possess, then, a very large number of texts of homilies given by Bonaventure. These have, however, survived in the manuscripts in various forms. Briefly stated there are three groups: (1) homilies which have been preserved in their full text—among these are the 50 *Sermones de Tempore* of 1250—1251, preached at Paris and edited by Bonaventure himself[33]—(2) homilies "reported" rather fully *(diffusius)* either by Bonaventure's own secretary or by those delegated with the responsibility of recording the

official homilies preached to the students at the university
—these usually contain the theme, the divisions with their
Scriptural supports, and some indication of the expansion
used—and (3) those reported very briefly *(brevius)*—these
are merely the bare schemata giving us only the Scripture
text, the divisions, and sometimes additional Scriptural confirmation; but we must imagine the expansion which Bonaventure uses in developing the theme. It is from the brief
headings in the various manuscripts of the homilies that we
have some information as to locale and congregation for
that occasion. Unfortunately, although the indication of the
Sunday or feastday is given, the year is not. Thus it is impossible to establish a full chronology for Bonaventure as
preacher. Fr. Bougerol[34] has outlined a probable sequence
for many of the full texts; but for the little schemata,
one can only surmise.

A small word about the selections chosen for this volume.
It is an attempt to be representative—if 15 from 700 can be
"representative"—representative of Bonaventure in his early
preaching of 1250 and his voice in 1273; representative of
the types of homilies as recorded in the manuscripts from
full text to fairly complete to mere outline; representative,
too, of various congregations and places, e.g., Franciscans,
Dominicans, students, people, Paris, Lyons, Assisi, etc.; representative of Bonaventure's insights both philosophical and
theological; representative of his expertise in rhetorical techniques and rhythmic prose; representative most of all of his
wisdom, knowledge, and mystical love that flows through
and bursts forth from his words inviting, enticing, reward-
ing us with a touch of the depth and joy of his close unity
with Father, Son, and Holy Spirit.

Troy, New York
14 June 1973   Marigwen Schumacher

NOTES

(1) I am following the chronology as established by Fr. Abate and adopted by Fr. Bougerol.

(2) Cf. Moorman, J. *A History of the Franciscan Order* (Oxford, 1968), chapter 13.

(3) Of special significance are the series of Lenten lectures given at Paris in 1267, 1268, and 1273. For estimates of his travels, see Moorman, *op. cit.*, p. 147, n.2.

(4) This is evidenced by the manuscript headings for his Letters and Homilies. Consult, also, Bougerol, J. Guy, *Introduction to the Works of Bonaventure* (Paterson, N.J., 1963; Chicago, Ill., 1971), p. 149.

(5) A complete, chronological listing is given on pages 129-130.

(6) Consult reports of the Council Proceedings from Lyons as well as the essay, "De Vita Seraphici Doctoris" found in vol. X of his *Opera Omnia*, Quaracchi.

(7) Cf. Bougerol, *op. cit.*, p. 149.

(8) Frequently there was also a "*Collatio*" or "Conference" in the evening after Vespers. Sometimes the manuscript indicates that a homily was given "to the Friars in Chapter."

(9) Only in 1215 did the Fourth Lateran Council approve a wider range of preachers.

(10) Cf. Clagett, M., Post, G., Reynolds, R., *Twelfth-Century Europe and the Foundations of Modern Society* (Madison, Wisconsin, 1966) and Deuchler, F., *The Year 1200:A Background Survey* (New York, 1970).

(11) Cf. Moorman, *op. cit.*, chapter 24.

(12) Bonaventure, *Explanation of the Rule of the Friars Minor*, chapter 9, 1-13.

(13) Bonaventure, *Opera Omnia*, vol. IX, p. 436.

(14) Bonaventure, *op. cit.*, IX. p. 575. Cf. also p. 281.

(15) Cited in the essay, "De Vita Seraphici Doctoris," *Opera Omnia*, X, p. 47.

(16) Sixtus V, *Triumphantis Ierusalem*, Opera Omnia, I, pp. xlvii ff.

(17) Alan de Lille, *Summa de arte praedicatoria*. P.L. 210, 111 ff.

(18) Clarke, M.L *Rhetoric at Rome—a historical survey* (London, 1953).

(19) Clarke, M.L. *op. cit.*, chapter 8.

(20) Baldwin, Charles S., *Mediaeval Rhetoric and Poetic* (Macmillan, 1928), p. 229.

(21) Bougerol, *op. cit.*, pp. 136-143 and Charland, Th. P. *Artes Praedicandi* (Ottawa, 1936), chapters 1 - 9.

(22) E.g. in the section of Homilies, consult #7 Love's Command and #14 Flowers.

(23) Charland, *op. cit.*, p. 136.

(24) Bonaventure, *op. cit.*, IX, p. 319. In ascensione Domini, sermo 3.

(25) *Ars Concionandi* is found in Bonaventure, *Opera Omnia*, IX, pp. 8 - 21. For further analysis of this treatise, consult the writer's article, "Bonaventure: The Power of Metaphor," *The Cord*, vol. XXI, no. 10 (Oct. 1970).

(26) Cf. *supra* p. 5 and references 15 and 16.

(27) Cf. Baldwin, *op. cit.*, *passim*.

(28) Baldwin, *op. cit.*, p. 110. Consult anthologies of early Latin verse

(29) Baldwin, *op. cit.*, p. 110.

(30) Kuhn, Sherman M., "Cursus in Old English: Rhetorical Ornament or Linguistic Phenomenon?," *Speculum*, used by Baldwin, *op. cit.*, p. 223.

(31) Baldwin, *op. cit.*, p. 225.

(32) Cf. Bibliography for complete listings.

(33) Bonaventure, *op. cit.*, IX, p. 404 and Bougerol, *op. cit.*, pp. 146 - 147.

(34) Bougerol, *op. cit.*, pp. 171 - 177.

Homilies

By St. Bonaventure

Three things are necessary to everyone regardless of status, sex, or age, i.e., truth of faith which brings understanding; love of Christ which brings compassion; endurance of hope which brings perseverance. No adult is in a state of salvation unless he has faithful understanding in his mind, loving compassion in his heart, and enduring perseverance in his actions.

—St. Bonaventure, *Homilies*

1

TRANSLATOR'S NOTE

The quotations from Scripture follow the translations of the Jerusalem Bible except in those places where their translation does not capture the word-play which Bonaventure is stressing. Whenever the Jerusalem Bible is not quoted, the translation of the Latin Scripture text used by Bonaventure has been substituted in the entire quotation or a part of it, and an asterisk is placed before the reference. Occasionally the quotations have been lengthened in order to complete the thought or more fully explain the reference which Bonaventure is making At times, Bonaventure interprets within the Scripture quotation: his added words are indicated by inclusions in brackets.

Quotations from Augustine, Aristotle, Gregory, *et al.* have been translated by the writer and references given according to the identifications indicated in the Quaracchi edition.

In my translations of Bonaventure's words, I have attempted as much as possible to capture the power of his expressions, his precision of word-choice, and his stylistic techniques, while at the same time striving to be accurate to his thought. Many times I have chosen to stress the *linguistic* meaning of a word or phrase rather than its standard pietistic or philosophical translation. This has been done deliberately to effect a freshness of contemporary phrasing and to force a re-consideration of the enduring vitality of Bonaventure's theological and homiletic statements.

Thanking God

I NEVER STOP THANKING GOD FOR ALL THE GRACES YOU HAVE RECEIVED through Jesus Christ. I thank him that you have been enriched in so many ways. . . . The witness to Christ has indeed been strong among you. *1 Cor 1:4-5*

The apostle Paul, in these words, explains for Christians, followers of God, (1) his own deep and unbounded interest in the salvation of others, and (2) the life-giving tendency of God to bless these same individuals. The first — "I never stop thanking God for all the graces you have received through Jesus Christ" — because you now honor God and firmly accept the life-style given us by Christ Jesus; the second is expressed — "I thank him that you have been enriched in so many ways." There is a richness of God's graces by which his gifts to us are increasingly piled high.

First of all, reflect that, as Paul says in his letters, we, too, should "never stop thanking God" for four special blessings:

(a) The blessing of creation.

He made us intelligent beings along with the angels — created to his image for his praise and glory:

God created man in the image of himself. *Gen 1:27*

Blessed be God the Father of our Lord Jesus Christ, who has blessed us with all the spiritual blessings of heaven in Christ. Before the world was made, he chose us . . . to live through love in his presence. *Eph 1:3*

Translator's Note: Bonaventure preached this homily [1] on the "18th Sunday after Pentecost" to the people of Lyons. It is an example of the "division extra" explained in the Introductory Essay. We can easily feel the impact of Bonaventure's emphasis on the richness of God's blessing's contrasted with our own poverty.

(b) The blessing of his guidance.

He guides us from inside and out and strengthens us in our suffering:

Blessed be the God and Father of our Lord Jesus Christ, a gentle Father and the God of all consolation, who comforts us in all our sorrows, so that we can offer others, in their sorrows, the consolation that we have received from God ourselves.   *2 Cor 1:3-4*

(c) The blessing of his invitation to us.

He has called us to faithfulness in grace and placed us amongst his chosen ones:

Declare his praise before the nations, you who are the sons of Israel! . . . Many nations shall come from far away, from all the ends of the earth, to dwell close to the holy name of the Lord God.   *Tob 13: 3, 14*

(d) The blessing of his ransoming us.

He redeemed us from the clutches of the devil, of sin, and of hell:

We have never failed to remember you in our prayers and to give thanks for you to God, the Father of our Lord Jesus Christ, ever since we heard about your faith in Christ Jesus and the love that you show towards all the saints because of the hope which is stored up for you in heaven.   *Col 1:3-4*

You say to yourself, "I am rich, I have made a fortune, and have everything I want," never realizing that you are wretchedly and pitiably poor, and blind and naked too. I warn you, buy from me the gold that has been tested in the fire to make you really rich, and white robes to clothe you and cover your shameful nakedness and eye ointment to put on your eyes so that you are able to see.   *Rev 3:17-18*

Mankind in separation from God is poverty-stricken because of failures; pitiable because of foolishness; blind from lack of knowledge; and naked because bereft of every blessing. On the other hand, in re-union with God, mankind is enriched with four-faceted riches in Christ Jesus. These alleviate that fourfold weakness noted above. Repentant sinners are enriched with the riches of compassion; those who pray deeply and preachers of the Gospel are enriched with the riches of wisdom; the innocent and just are enriched with the riches of grace; the angels and those blessed who come to "know" God are enriched with the riches of glory. Therefore, one who is poverty-stricken from failure becomes rich in the treasury of compassion; one who is blind from lack of knowledge is made rich from the treasury of wisdom; one who is naked from the lack of blessings becomes rich in the treasure-house of grace; one who is pitiable from his lack of security becomes rich in the treasury of glory. In these four ways the four harmful dimensions of poverty which are in the world are removed through these four outstanding riches which are found in the Lord Jesus Christ.

If we, then, are poverty-stricken from our failures, let us turn around and be made rich in that treasury of compassion:

But God loved us with so much love that he was generous with his mercy; when we were dead through our sins, he brought us to life with Christ. *Eph 2:4-5*

If we are blind from lack of knowledge, let us turn around and be made rich in that treasure-house of wisdom:

I have been made the servant of that gospel by a gift of grace from God who gave it to me by his own power. I . . . have been entrusted with this special grace not only of proclaiming to the pagans the infinite treasure of Christ but also of explaining how the mystery is to be dispensed. *Eph 3:7-9*

If we are naked from the lack of blessings, let us turn and become rich in that treasury of graces:

He determined that we should become his adopted sons through Jesus Christ, for his own kind of purposes, to make us praise the glory of his grace, his free gift to us in the Beloved, in whom, through his blood, we gain our freedom, the forgiveness of sins. Such is the richness of the grace which has been showered on us. *Eph 1:5-6*

If we are pitiable from our lack of security, let us nourish deep desires for salvation so that we become rich from that treasure-house of glory:

May the God of our Lord Jesus Christ, the Father of glory, give you a spirit of wisdom and perception of what is revealed to bring you to full knowledge of him. May he

NOTE

(1) Bonaventure, *Opera Omnia*, IX, pp. 425 - 426: Dom. XVIII post Pentecosten - sermo 2.

Homily 2

Prayer

〰〰〰〰〰〰〰〰〰〰〰〰〰〰〰〰〰〰〰〰〰〰

MY HOUSE WILL BE A HOUSE OF PRAYER.   *Lk 19:46*

These I will bring to my holy mountain. I will make them joyful in my house of prayer . . . my house will be called a house of prayer for all the peoples.   *Is 56:7*

In this text, the Lord describes the place of his in-dwelling through the action of prayer. Two points are noteworthy: first, the place of his dwelling is advanced as "well-known," i.e., "my house"; second, the action of prayer is referred to as "making known," i.e., "will be a house of prayer." In this unique manner both his dwelling and our prayer are emphasized. The house of God has such an exceptional quality that God does not accept there any action other than of prayer. Then again, prayer is exceptional so that for it especially and particularly the divine dwelling has been made ready. If, therefore, this "being known" quality of the house of divine in-dwelling is correct, then no one faithfully and endlessly remains in the house of God unless he concentrates on prayer. Likewise everyone who earnestly and perseveringly devotes himself to prayer stays in the house of God. And this is proper for he alone is ready for salvation. Therefore, the whole effort of our salvation stresses the proper and consistent practice of prayer. In this regard, there are three things necessary for prayer to be pleasing and welcome to God. These are:

Translator's Note: Bonaventure preached this homily[1] in Paris at the house of the Dominicans on the "9th Sunday after Pentecost." We find here a very beautiful meditation on prayer explained through a metaphor-progression from "scrubbing," i.e., "making ready" to "brightening," i.e., "attentiveness" to "polishing," i.e., "passionate joy."

I. A "making ready" must lead the way to prayer.

II. Attentiveness must accompany prayer.

III. Passionate joy must follow close after prayer.

These correspond to the three actions of prayer: scrubbing, brightening, and polishing.

I. First of all, because of the exceptional nature of the action, it is reasonable that a "scrub-up" precede:

Prepare yourself before making a vow, and do not be like a man who tempts the Lord.   *Sir 18:23*

The person needs to be scrubbed clean from the three sources of all squalor:

(1) from stubborn pride — this is cleansed through gentle acceptance; (2) from sensual amusement — through bitter remorse; (3) from frenzied activity — through a reverent aloneness.

These three obviously correspond to the other three.

(1) First, then, the person must be scrubbed clean from stubborn pride to be ready for prayer:

He who turns his ear away from listening to the Law, his prayer is an abomination.   *Prov 28:9*

The reason is that whoever "does not listen to the Divine Law" and rejects God, God does not listen to him because "in whatever manner a man brings himself to God, in the same manner God presents himself to him." [2] The prayer of the proud man is not hearable but detestable. Therefore, whoever wishes to be listened to should be cleansed from his pride. This is accomplished through gentle surrender:

Since you are the God of the humble, the help of the oppressed, the support of the weak, the refuge of the forsaken, the savior of the despairing. Please, please, God of my father, God of the heritage of Israel, Master of heaven and earth, Creator of the waters, King of your whole creation, hear my prayer.   *Jdt 9:16-18*

Again:

The humble man's prayer pierces the clouds, because it ascends to the divine gaze. Therefore: *Sir 35:21*

He will answer the prayer of the abandoned, he will not scorn their petitions.   *Ps 102:17*

Meditate on the story of the tax-collector as told in Luke 18, 9-14.

(2) Second, the person must be scrubbed clean from sensual amusement through keen repentance:

When you stretch out your hands I turn my eyes away. You may multiply your prayers, I shall not listen. Your hands are covered with blood, wash, make yourselves clean.
Is 1:15-16

The sensual, pleasure-loving person, as though mired in the mud, shapes earthy heavy words within himself. He does not gain what he seeks because his prayers are not brought by the hands of the Angels to God's attention. Therefore, it is fitting for one who wishes to be heard to be cleansed through poignant repentance:

When Anna was bitter in spirit, she prayed to Yahweh with many tears . . . *1 Sam 1:10*

Through her weeping she purified herself and, as it were, washed in the spring. Then from her lips seemly prayer rose up all the way to heaven and was heard. This is depicted in Judith:

She went out each night to the valley of Bethulia and washed at the spring. . . . As she came up again, she prayed to the Lord God of Israel to guide her in her plan to relieve the children of her people. *Jdt 12:7-8*

This is to symbolize that our consciousness must be washed night after night.

I am worn out with groaning, every night I drench my pillow and soak my bed with tears, *Ps 6:7*

before we rise to prayer. Consider the example of Esther praying. *Cf. Esther 14:1-17*

(3) Third, the person must be scrubbed clean from frenzied activity through a reverent aloneness so that he may be available and open to prayer:

You have wrapped yourself in a cloud too thick for prayer to pierce. *Lam 3:44*

This indeed happens whenever we allow our heart to be so wound up in vague imaginings and business tensions that we cannot give attention to the beam of true light. As long as our mind is caught up in these phantasies and destructive tensions, it is drawn far away from truth and spirit. As a result, it cannot pray properly because:

God is Spirit and those who worship must worship in spirit and in truth.   *Jn 4:24*

Our mind, then, must be freed from these distractions. This is accomplished by a reverent aloneness, i.e., by withdrawing from the crowd of sensations, real and imaginary. This is well shown in Matthew where it is said that the Savior,

after sending the crowds away, went up into the hills by himself to pray.   *Mt 14:23*

This reverent aloneness (i.e., "at-one-ness") is more easily achieved through a spiritual withdrawal into the interior consciousness than through a physical separation from the fellowship of the crowd:

But when you pray go to your private room and, when you have shut the door, pray to your Father who is in that secret place.   *Mt 6:6*

The "door," i.e., of the exterior senses, for there is the heart of man. But there are few who walk in because this is a gift of divine grace and of our attentiveness:

Your servant entered into his heart that he might pray to you with this prayer . . .   *2 Sam 7:27*

Consider, too, the prayer of Sara.   *Cf. Tob 3:11-16*

II. When this threefold scrubbing has been completed as a "making ready," prayer must be joined with attentiveness as a companion. This too should be moulded of three qualities:

(1) Prayer must be attentive with a foreseeing alertness through a wakeful understanding, e.g.

You should be awake and praying not to be put to the test . . .   *Mt 26:41*

Wait here and keep awake . . . the spirit is willing but the flesh is weak.   *Mk 14:34, 38*

Watch yourselves, or your hearts will be coarsened with

debauchery and drunkenness and the cares of life, and that day will be sprung on you suddenly, like a trap. For it will come down on every living man on the face of the earth. Stay awake, praying at all times for the strength to survive all that is going to happen, and to stand with confidence before the Son of Man. *Lk 21:34-36*

To pray better, keep a calm and sober mind. *1 Pet 4:7*

This is taught by the Lord either because of the deceitfulness of the enemy:

Be calm but viligant, because your enemy the devil . . .
1 Pet 5:8

or because of the intensity of our longing:

You are my God . . . I invoke you all day long; give your servant reason to rejoice . . . Yahweh, hear my prayer, listen to me as I plead. *Ps 86:3-5*

or because of the impatient haste of the Bridegroom who comes quickly and at an undefined time:

Happy those servants whom the master finds awake when he comes. *Lk 12:37*

or because of our dire poverty:

At dawn and with all his heart (the just man) resorts to the Lord who made him; he pleads in the presence of the Most High, he opens his mouth in prayer and makes entreaty for his sins. *Sir 39:6-7*

Christ taught us this as Luke says:

Now it was about this time that he went into the hills to pray; and he spent the whole night in prayer to God.
Lk 6:12

(2) Prayer must be reciprocal in friendliness and compassion:

So confess your sins to one another, and pray for one another, and this will cure you; the heartfelt prayer of a good man works very powerfully. *Jas 5:16*

"For one another" he says so that prayer extends itself in friendliness not only to friends but also to outsiders and enemies:

Love your enemies and pray for those who persecute you.

Mt 5:44

As Gregory says, "the penitent merits to be heard quickly on his own behalf in proportion as he devotedly intercedes for others." [3]   Jerome explains that "prayer is a small, delicate, little bird which by the wings of faith and virtue transcends the choirs of Cherubim and Seraphim and stands in the council hall of the Great King as a distinguished pleader for each and every one." Therefore:

You should all agree among yourselves and be sympathetic; love the brothers, have compassion.   **1 Pet 3:8*

"Have compassion" in prayer so that you shut out no one. This example Christ gave when he prayed for his executioners.   *Lk 23:34*

(3) Prayer must be uninterrupted and with constancy in action:

Let nothing prevent your discharging a vow in good time. And do not wait till death before setting matters to rights.

Sir 18:22

Therefore, if the Lord wished some things to happen at certain times, he also wished that prayer never cease:

Then he told them a parable about the need to pray continually and never lose heart.   *Lk 18:1*

Be happy at all times; pray constantly; and for all things give thanks to God, because this is what God expects you to do in Christ Jesus.   *1 Thess 5:17*

Again Gregory says "prayer which by no means aims to be continued through unceasing love does not have the weight of virtue." [4]   The explanation of this is that the beginning, the middle, and the end of a good work is through the gift of divine grace. This gift cannot be acquired unless one perseveringly pounds at the door:

Persistence will be enough to make him get up and give his friend all he wants.   *Lk 11:8*

III. Passionate joy ought to follow close after prayer for its polishing. This joy is welcome and is an awareness of blessing:

Be persevering in your prayers and be thankful as you stay awake to pray.
Col 4:2

This exuberant joy develops from the enjoyment of Presence:

Your prayer has been heard . . . will be your joy and delight . . .
Lk 1:13

Finally, this joy must be alive with that deep sense of protection:

In the daytime may Yahweh command his love to come, and by night may his song be on my lips, a prayer to the God of my life!
Ps 42:8

and also:

Your love is better than life itself, my lips will recite your praise; all my life I will bless you, in your name, lift up my hands; my soul will feast most richly, on my lips a song of joy and in my mouth, praise. On my bed I think of you, I meditate on you all night long, for you have always helped me. I sing for joy in the shadow of your wings; my soul clings close to you, your right hand supports me.
Ps 63:3-8

Let us ask the Lord that He grant us this. . . .

NOTES

(1) Bonaventure, *op. cit.*, IX, pp. 390 - 392: Dom. IX post Pentecosten - sermo 2.
(2) Bernard, *sermo* 69 *in Cant.*, n. 7.
(3) Gregory, *Moral.* XXXV, c. 11, n. 21.
(4) Gregory, *Moral.* XXXIII, c. 23, n. 43.

Six Days

SIX DAYS BEFORE THE PASSOVER, JESUS WENT TO BETHANY

John 12, 1

This text carefully points out for us the pathway of our salvation. There are three considerations: (1) the directness of the journey, i.e., "six days before"; (2) the benefit of achieving the goal, i.e., "Passover"; (3) the good sense of the guide, i.e., "Jesus".

Apropos of the first point, reflect that the "six days" are to be understood as that spiritual training related to the six insights which the spiritual sun shining in through the presence of grace, accomplishes in our spirit:

I. The first is embarrassment in remembering our disgraceful deeds:

All day long I brood on this disgrace, my face covered in shame.   *Ps 44:15*

This is the result of wholesome remorse, acknowledgment, and offerings. Or it comes from the greatness of our sins since they our the greater in proportion to the importance of the One offended; or from the multitude of our sins since the sinner misuses all things; or from their disgraceful ugliness since the spirit which is the most beautiful of creation becomes the ugliest through sin. This day corresponds

---

Translator's Note: This homily [1] was given on the Monday of Holy Week. Expanding on the opening words of the text, Bonaventure interprets the "six days" as the "six insights" for growth in spirituality. We find the same expansion in chapter 3, section 2 of his *De Triplici Via* which was written in 1259 after his experience on Alverna. This theme of "six days" was a favored one with Bonaventure. It would seem from the closing section with its interpretation of "Bethany" that Bonaventure was here preaching to the Friars.

to the first day of creation in which there was light.

Cf. Gen 1:3

Just as a person is not ashamed in the night but in the day, so the sinner at openness.

II. The second is fear of the consequences of judgment:

From the depths of day I will fear but I will hope in you.

*Ps 56:4

i.e., from the bottomless depths of judgment which will be unmistakable, unchangeable, inescapable. "Unmistakable" because nothing will be able to be concealed from the judge. "Unchangeable" because no one will be able to appeal the verdict. "Inescapable" because no one will be able to flee. This day corresponds to the second day on which

the vault of the heavens was made, **Gen 1:6*

dividing the waters above the vault from those below. So fear of judgment stabilizes a man in good and shelters him from the turmoil of worldly attractions.

III. The third is chagrin on reflecting upon what he has lost:

Bowed down, bend double, overcome, I go mourning all the day. *Ps 38:6*

This is the result of the loss of divine grace or friendship and the injury of human nature from the loss of its previous life. This corresponds to the third day on which

dry land appeared, producing seed-bearing plants and fruit-bearing trees. **Gen 1:9, 11*

The human heart, as long as it is covered with the waters of worldly concerns, can have no integrity nor produce the fruit of good actions.

IV. The fourth is outcry in appealing for assistance:

You are my God, take pity on me Lord, I invoke you all day long; give your servant reason to rejoice, for to you, Lord, I lift my soul. *Ps 86:3-4*

Each one must shout and cry out — sometimes to the Trinity for help, sometimes to the Blessed Virgin for protection, sometimes to the whole Church triumphant for aid.

This day corresponds to the fourth day on which

were made the lights in the vault of heaven   *Gen 1:14

because then are obtained the charismatic graces, i.e., wisdom for prayerfulness, discretion for life's guidance, and strength for the power of action. These three are understood by "sun, moon, and stars."

V. The fifth is firmness in controlling temptation:

It is for your sake we are being massacred daily, and counted as sheep for the slaughter.   *Ps 44:22*

This is accomplished by self-discipline towards spiritual emptiness, carnal lusts, and wordly allurements. This corresponds to the fifth day on which

were produced the fish in the seas   *Gen 1:20

which die when extracted from these waters. So, too, a Religious is immediately spiritually dead when he goes beyond the limits of his chosen life-style.

VI. The sixth is eagerness and passionate longing for the Beloved:

My beloved is mine and I am his. He pastures his flock among the lilies before the dawn-winds rise, before the shadows flee.   *Song 2:16-17*

This is the sixth day and the sixth hour in which the Beloved not only is loved but also loves and shows his love in a wonderful way. It was

from the sixth hour   *Mt 27:45*

that Christ suffered on the cross.

Tell me then, you whom my heart loves: Where will you lead your flock to graze. Where will you rest it at noon? That I may no more wander like a vagabond beside the flocks of your companions.   *Song 1:7*

This corresponds to the sixth day on which

mankind was made in the image of God and put in charge of the beasts on the earth and other creatures.   *Gen 1:26

Through this eagerness and intense longing for God the spirit becomes "God-like" and heart and mind govern, as far as is possible, all baser sensual drives.

Afterwards follows the seventh day, i.e., Passover which can be called "repose." This is restfulness in God — viewing and enjoying His divine sweetness:

A single day in your courts is worth more than a thousand elsewhere; merely to stand on the steps of God's house, is better than living with the wicked.   *Ps 84:10*

Notice, too, that this was in "Bethany" which is interpreted as "house of obedience, house of affliction, house of the gift of God, house pleasing to the Lord." Rightly through this is to be understood the spirit of B. Francis concerning obedience. Obedience is expected without conflict of will, without murmur in speech, without delay in action.

Likewise it is a house of self-restraint. There chastity is offered to God. In this gift there are understood to be certain essentials, such as, avoidance of all physical seduction both in action and in desire; certain supports, such as, a number 'of harsh practices; certain remedies, such as, escape from mistrusted fellowship.

But it is called "pleasing to God" through poverty. Where there is greed or ownership in a Religious, there not God but an idol is being worshiped. Real and complete poverty requires: taking nothing for oneself; having or keeping nothing; giving or receiving nothing without permission from the master.

Let us ask the Lord. . . .

NOTE

(1) Bonaventure, *op. cit.*, IX, pp. 246 - 247; feria secunda post Dom. in palmis - sermo. Cf. also Bougerol, *op. cit.*, p. 162 and p. 230 n. 55.

He Will Lead

$$\approx\!\!\sim\!\!\sim\!\!\sim\!\!\sim\!\!\sim\!\!\sim\!\!\sim\!\!\sim\!\!\sim\!\!\sim\!\!\sim\!\!\sim\!\!\sim\!\!\sim\!\!\sim\!\!\sim\!\!\sim\!\!\sim$$

HE WHO WALKS AT THEIR HEAD WILL LEAD THE WAY IN FRONT OF THEM: he will walk at their head, they will pass through the gate.

Mic 2:13

In these brief words, the prophet Micah understands the two facets of the mystery of today's celebration:

(1) the "raising up" of human nature — "he who walks at their head will lead; (2) the "opening up" of heaven — "in front of them . . . they will pass through the gate."

(1) Micah asserts "he will lead the way" but not only by himself: there will be others after him for the Prophet adds "in front of them." "He will lead the way in front of them": (a) to give direction; (b) to enkindle; (c) to encourage; (d) to make preparations for lodging and entertainment.

(a) He gives right direction to those who are seriously considering — so that they "see" correctly. (b) He enkindles those who are starting out — so that they have courage to really get underway. (c) He encourages those who are already actively involved — so that they have strength to continue on to the end. (d) He prepares lodging and entertainment for those who steadfastly complete the journey —so that they rejoice in everlasting joy.

(a) He leads the way in front of them to give directions or to explain the road. "He will lead the way in front of them," i.e., showing them the road. The road of life was

---

Translator's Note: This is one of Bonaventure's homilies for the feast of the Ascension.[1] It is carefully structured to stress not only Christ as leader on the road but the followers and their various situations, e.g., beginners, strangers, etc., and the particular guidance which each needs, e.g., enkindle, encourage, etc.

unknown before Christ Jesus walked before us; but he has

revealed to us the paths of life   *Ps 16:11*

i.e., justice, compassion, truth. It is by these roads that we come to life says Augustine in a sermon on the Resurrection. Likewise:

Yahweh went before them, by day in the form of a pillar of cloud to show them the way, and by night in the form of a pillar of fire to give them light: thus they could continue their march by day and by night.   *Ex 13:21*

Note that he walked just as one who carries a torch at night in front of important people.

(b) He leads the way in front to enkindle them. This was prefigured when:

Moses said "If you are not going with us yourself, do not make us leave this place. By what means can it be known that I, I and my people, have won your favor, if not by your going with us? . . . " Yahweh said to Moses, "Again, I will do what you have asked . . . "   *Ex 33:15-17*

The road was dangerous and the shoals deep and, therefore, he walked before them to test the fording places. It was necessary to cross over through a troubled stream which was not sufficiently safe. Consider the symbol of this in the incident of Timotheus and Judas:

Judas then advanced to engage them, and was approaching the watercourse with his troops when Timotheus told the commanders of his army, "If he crosses first we shall not be able to resist him, because he will have the advantage of us . . . " Judas himself was the first across to the enemy side, with all the people following.

1 Macc 5:40, 43

(c) He leads the way in front to encourage them — just as travellers who are stronger are wont to go ahead of the others beyond the boundary-line and stretch forth their hands to help them:

He rides the heavens to your rescue, rides the clouds in his majesty. The God of old, he is your refuge.   *Deut 33:26*

I myself taught Ephraim to walk, I took them in my arms; . . . I led them with reins of kindness, with leading strings of love.   *Hos 11:3-4*

Likewise when Peter began to sink

Jesus put out his hand at once and held him.   *Mt 14:30*

(d) He leads the way in front of them to prepare lodgings and entertainment:

I am going now to prepare a place for you, and after I have gone and prepared you a place, I shall return to take you with me; so that where I am you may be too.   *Jn 14:2-4*

He leads the way in front of them for these four reasons. He accomplished the first in conversations, the second in suffering, the third in resurrection, and the fourth in ascending. As a result of the first, we ought to be sagacious in choosing; from the second, daring in setting forth; from the third, vigorous in pressing on; from the fourth, eager to finish so that we can, after our activities are completed, enter into that lodging which has been prepared for us and in which all good things have also been made ready for us:

Everything is ready. Come!   *Mt 22:5*

(2) Consequently,

we must do everything we can to reach that place of rest.
                                                        Heb 4:11

especially when we see today's "opening up" and so many entering in to the festival. Reflect upon those who are going in to the feast! But since entry into the kingdom is not given to everyone who knocks on the door:

It is not those who say to me, "Lord, Lord," who will enter the kingdom of heaven, but the person who does the will of my Father in heaven.   *Mt 7:21-22*

we must take precautions to be the sort to whom entrance is granted following the Lord who today "leads the way in front of" his people. Let us see to it that we are recognized as members of his family or his people:

For Yahweh has not abandoned or deserted his hereditary people.   *Ps 94:14*

A person is acknowledged as a member of some distinguished family in various ways. Sometimes the person declares himself to be that man's follower. Sometimes he studies his writings. Sometimes he dwells with him. Sometimes he wears clothes made from the same materials. The first group symbolizes the declaration of faith of the laity; the second, the knowledge of the clergy; the third, the at-one-ness of the Religious; and the fourth, the imitation of the saints.

(a) Some, then, are recognized by the Lord and welcomed into his home because they declare themselves to be his followers:

I tell you, if anyone openly declares himself for me in the presence of men, the Son of Man will declare himself for him in the presence of God's angels. *Lk 12:8*

But watch out! Often the one declaring himself for another is unknown unless he wears "his campaign buttons":

Take the case, my brothers, of someone who has never done a single good act but claims that he has faith. Will that faith save him? *Jas 2:14*

as though he says "NO!" because he does not have his full credentials:

They claim to have knowledge of God but the things they are doing are nothing but a denial of him. *Tit 1:16*

Consider the anecdote of the clergyman from whom it was asked, "what are your actions?"

(b) Some are welcomed because they study the Scriptures of the Lord: — Without this, clergy are not welcomed! —

As you have rejected knowledge so do I reject you from my priesthood; you have forgotten the teaching of your God. *Hos 4:6*

Likewise:

This is the book of the Commandments of God, the Law that stands forever; those who keep her live, those who desert her die. *Bar 4:1*

In this manner Paul writes to Timothy:

Ever since you were a child, you have known the Holy Scriptures — from these you can learn the wisdom that leads to salvation through faith in Christ Jesus.   *2 Tim 3:15*

Remember the anecdote about Jerome.

Consider, moreover, that in Scripture-study there ought to be the seal of love; otherwise it is not valid.

Set me like a seal on your heart, like a seal on your arm.   *Song 8:6*

Note that seal! On the other hand, this seal is not found with those hypocrites who are fakers and show a sham repentance. Reflect, too, how this happens to be discovered in them.

(c) Some are welcomed because they stay with him and are of his fellowship, i.e., those who have left all things for Christ Jesus:

You are the men who have stood by me faithfully in my trials; and now I confer a kingdom on you, just as my Father conferred one on me: you will eat and drink at my table in my kingdom, and you will sit on thrones to judge the twelve tribes of Israel.   *Lk 22:28-30*

and also:

If a man serves me, he must follow me, wherever I am, my servant will be there too.   *Jn 12:26*

It is also said of him "Go, sell what you have . . . and come follow me!" — and "where I am, there will my servant be also."

(d) Some are welcomed because they are dressed in clothes like his and these ought to be given greater respect. These are those who pattern themselves upon his suffering — which indicates the saints:

Happy are those who will have washed their robes clean, in the blood of the Lamb, so that they will have the right to feed on the tree of life and can come through the gates into the city.   **Rev 22:14*

Note the manner in which we are all dressed in the same clothes with him but we are not all dyed with the same color.

After him, then, are entering the laity faithfully declaring him; the clergy truthfully preaching him; the Religious steadfastly accompanying him; and the saints who have vibrantly moulded themsleves to his suffering.

May this be granted unto us! Amen!

NOTE

(1) Bonaventure, *op. cit.*, IX, pp. 326 - 327: In ascensione Domini - sermo 9.

Fire

〰〰〰〰〰〰〰〰〰〰〰〰〰〰〰〰〰〰〰〰〰〰〰〰〰〰

HE HAS SENT A FIRE FROM ON HIGH DOWN INTO MY BONES: AND HE
has perfected me.   *Lam 1:13*

This text is taken from the Book of Lamentations. In it
the Church reflects upon service given to her in this festival
of Pentecost. This gift of the Holy Spirit was given to the
Apostles, founders and teachers of the Church. There are
three considerations to be drawn from this text clarifying
this service: (1) the bountiful generosity of the Divine Giver,
i.e., "He has sent a fire from on high." "He," of course,
is the Lord on high. (2) the Church as receiver of this
gift, i.e., "down into my bones." The Apostles are called
"bones" because they support the Church just as our bones
support the building which is our body. (3) the finished
perfection, i.e., "and he had perfected me." That was the
fruit of this sending forth.

The text, then, is "He has sent a fire from on high."
Consider that there is fire which the Lord sends "from on
high," i.e., the fire of grace. There is also fire which he
allows to be enkindled from the depths, i.e., the fire of
guilt. There is, too, the fire which he sends along a middle
path, i.e., the fire of repentance.

Concerning the fire of grace which He sends from on high:

Translator's Note: Bonaventure preached this homily [1] on the feast of
Pentecost as he mentions at the beginning. His choice of a text from Lamentations reflects the variability of Scripture readings at that time. Although, in the opening passage, he explicitly divides the theme into three
sections, Bonaventure expands upon only the first one — that of "fire being
sent" — in his reflections. Throughout the various considerations of (1) the
fire of grace, (2) the fire of guilt, and (3) the fire of repentance, the imagery
of "fire" is sustained through many images and vignettes. The total impact of the homily is truly fire-bright and dazzling.

I have come to bring fire to the earth, and how I wish it were blazing already! *Lk 12:49*

Concerning the fire of guilt which is enkindled from below:

I it was created the smith who blows on the coal fire.

Is 54:16

The smith is the devil who blows to enkindle the fire of sin.

Concerning the fire of repentance which the Lord imposes:

You tested us, God. You refined us in the fire. **Ps 66:10*

I. First, then, we should reflect upon the fire of grace which the Lord "sends from on high." When we consider the properties of fire, we realize that it is an accurate description of grace. Fire has brightness in appearance, warmness of effect, quickness of movement. In the same way, grace shines because of knowledge, warms through love, enkindles and moves as a result of prayerfulness.

(a) Grace shines because of the knowledge through which God provides light for our eyes and shows us the path stretching homewards. This was well signified in Exodus where it is said of the sons of Israel:

Yahweh went before them, by day in the form of a pillar of cloud to show them the way, and by night in the form of a pillar of fire to give them light. *Ex 13:21*

By "night" is signified our present situation of misfortunes. The Lord directs and enlightens us through this gift, the light of grace.

(b) Grace warms through love. It is through love that God arouses our hearts:

Love is strong as Death, jealousy relentless as Sheol. The flash of it is a flash of fire, a flame of Yahweh himself. Love no flood can quench, no torrents drown. *Song 8:6-7*

Love, through grace, is correctly called "a flash of fire" and a "flame" because it inflames the heart on the inside with yearning and from the outside by example. Appropriately, too, is added "love no flood can quench." Actually — and this is really remarkable — the floods of distress enkindle this love:

In the very heart of the water [which extinguishes every-thing] the flame would burn more fiercely than fire.

Wis 16:19

(c) Grace stretches and moves upwards as a result of prayerfulness which lifts the heart towards higher aims. It is, accurately called "fire":

Then the angel of Yahweh reached out the tip of the staff in his hand and touched the meat and unleavened cakes. Fire sprang from the rock and consumed the meat and unleavened cakes.   *Judg 6:21*

That "angel" is Christ who is the "Angel of great counsel."   *Is 9:6*

The "staff" is his cross. He "reached out" with this when he projected his Passion. The "rock" is our hearts which, by themselves, are unyielding. Fire, indeed, "springs from the rock" from the reaching out of the staff whenever any person is wholly opened up in prayerfulness through reflection upon the Passion. At that moment our hearts are encouraged, through the fire of love, and climb upwards. Nor is this surprising since fire reaches towards the place of fire which is above:

It is Yahweh who speaks, whose fire is in Zion, and his furnace in Jerusalem.   *Is 31:9*

As a result, "the meat was consumed," i.e., carnal lusts, since, to quote Bernard, "when one has tasted of the spirit, all flesh becomes tasteless." [2]

Without this fire, there is no life. Consequently everyone should exert himself in order to possess this. Those who are without it are robbed of that light which directs, the warmth that arouses, the quickness and strength which leads up-wards.

Remember, then, that this fire of grace which is sent "from on high" is (a) enkindled in the patient; (b) nourished in the travelers; and (c) perfected in the beholders.

(a) It is enkindled in the patient through their rejection of sins. The Lord descends upon them:

The mountain of Sinai was entirely wrapped in smoke, because Yahweh had descended on it in the form of fire.

Ex 19:18

"Entirely" is well chosen because:

In the fire of his zeal will be devoured the whole earth.

*Zeph 1:18

i.e. all earthly attractions.

The "fire of divine zeal" is the fire of hatred for sin; God detests only evil. In this fire "will be devoured the whole earth," i.e., all earthly attractions and all guilt. It is clear from this that anyone who wishes to have this fire of divine grace in himself must pursue it in all ways and through all means. He must also hate all causes of guilt in himself and in others. Note that this is first "in himself" and then "in others"; and first and especially in those greater causes for guilt, then in the lesser ones.

(b) It is nourished in travelers through their fulfilling his precepts. Good actions relate to love just as firewood to fire:

The fire . . . on the altar must not be allowed to go out. The priest must nourish it every day in the morning by adding more wood. **Lev 6:12*

"Wood" must always "be added" just as good actions must always be completed and divine precepts continuously heeded:

If you love me you will keep my commandments. *Jn 14:15*

Just as a fire cannot continue without more wood, neither can the grace of God which is love without good actions. As Gregory comments, "there is great activity where there is love; if one refuses to be active, then love is not present." [3] Previously he says that "Love for God is never idle." Just as good actions nourish the fire of love between us and God, so, too, a gentle disposition nourishes it between us and our neighbor, both those who are friendly and those who are unfriendly:

If your enemy is hungry, you should give him food, and if he is thirsty, let him drink. Thus you heap red-hot coals on his head. *Rom 12:20*

(c) This fire is perfected in the beholders through their reflection upon the Lord's generosity:

My heart had been smoldering inside me, [from remembrance of my sins] but it flared up at the thought of this . . . [i.e. reflection upon divine generosity].   *Ps 39:3*

Who has a heart so unyielding that, when he reflects and considers the generosity which the Lord manifests in creation, in redemption, in calling us individually, in the promise of future glory, he is not wholly touched and transformed into love for God? If, therefore, anyone wishes to have this grace perfected in him, he must be pleasing to God. For how can grace abound in one who is displeasing to God? And how can one be "pleasing" if he does not consider the gifts which God so freely has given? Let us, then, weep for our sins; let us fulfill those divine precepts and reflect upon his gifts so generously given to us. Thus may the fire of grace be enkindled in us, nourished, and perfected. May Our Lord himself graciously provide this for us . . .

II. Opposite to this fire of grace is the fire of guilt. This fire does not come "from on high" since the devil enkindles it from the depths. Therefore, this fire is not of heaven but of earth. Its smokiness beclouds, its ravenousness devours, its violence molests those three qualities of which we have just spoken.

(a) That smoky fire which beclouds is that uncertainty of conscience which closes our eys to the fickleness of this life:

Fire fell upon them and they did not see the sun.   *Ps 57:9*

The fire which closes the eyes of the mind and keeps it from seeing the sun is that uncertainty of consicence; this so beclouds itself that it considers light to be present in darkness and, contrariwise, light as darkness:

Woe to those who call evil good, and good evil, who substitute darkness for light and light for darkness!   *Is 5:20*

The devil cheerfully enkindles this fire: he does it especially through malicious people:

You are well aware, then, that anybody who tries to live in devotion to Christ is certain to be attacked; while these wicked imposters will go from bad to worse, deceiving others and deceived themselves. *2 Tim 3:13*

This was clearly pre-figured:

Samson went off and caught 300 foxes, then took torches and turning the foxes tail to tail put a torch between each pair of tails. He lit the torches and set the foxes free, so that they would run about hither and thither. **Judg 15:4-5*

What is to be understood by "foxes" other than cunning men who have "fire at their tails" because, to the very end, they are running headlong into error.

(b) That ravenous fire which devours is the passion of carnal desires:

There are three insatiable things, four, indeed, that never say, "Enough!" Sheol, the barren womb, earth which can never have its fill of water, fire which never says, "Enough."! *Prov 30:16*

That, I say, is the fire both of desires of the body and desires of the eyes. This fire of carnal lust completely devours everything yet is not satiated:

If I ever lost my heart to any woman, or lurked at my neighbor's door, let my wife grind corn that is not mine, let her sleep between other's sheets. For I should have committed a sin of lust, a crime punishable by the law, and should have lit a fire burning till Perdition, which would have devoured all my harvesting. *Job 31:9-12*

It utterly destroys everything because it takes away those gifts of body and spirit, innate and freely given, life and honor, God and oneself. Thus it destroys everything that is worthwhile. The fire of greed, i.e., desires of the eyes, is similar:

The eye of the grasping man is not content with his portion, greed shrivels up the soul. *Sir 14:9*

"Greed shrivels up the soul" due to an excessive drive of desires:

There is a desire that, blazing like a furnace, cannot be quenched until it is slaked. There is a man who lusts for his own flesh: he will not give up until the fire consumes him.   *Sir 23:22-23*

This thirst, then, is like the thirst of a man with dropsy; it is increased by drinking rather than quenched.

(c) That violent fire which molests is the fury of anger:

A scoundrel digs deep for mischief-making, on his lips is a fire that scorches.   *Prov 16:27*

The "fire" which "scorches" in the mouth of the scoundrel is the fury of anger. A small word of anger enkindles a mighty fire of fury:

Think how small a flame can set fire to a huge forest; the tongue is a flame like that. Among all the parts of the body, the tongue is a whole wicked world in itself: it infects the whole body; catching fire itself from hell, it sets fire to the whole wheel of creation.   *Jas 3:5-6*

A hearthful of glowing coals starts from a single spark, and the sinner lurks for the chance to spill blood.   *Sir 11:34*

This fire is found especially amongst wrongdoers and is there enkindled:

A meeting of lawless men is like a heap of hemp; they will end in a blazing fire.   *Sir 21:10*

The reason for this is that they are impatient and thus easily angered — just as hemp is easily burned.

Through this fire of guilt, the mind of the unfortunate sinner is beclouded, devoured, and molested. This fire, therefore, should be quenched. Remember that actual fires are put out in three different ways: (1) by removing the wood, (2) by pouring on water, (3) by the blasts of wind.

(1) In the same way, the fire of guilt is quenched by removing the wood, i.e., by avoiding those favorable moments. Such moments are like firewood.   *Prov 26:20*

No wood, and the fire goes out; no talebearer, and the quarrelling dies down.   *Prov 26:20*

The reason for this is that nasty, quarrelsome words feed the fire of fury:

Do not quarrel with a man of quick tongue, do not pile logs on his fire.   *Sir 6:3*

Anyone who wishes to quench the fire of desires ought to do the same:

Keep your eyes to yourself in the streets of a town, do not prowl about its unfrequented quarters. Turn your eyes away from a handsome woman, do not stare at the beauty that belongs to someone else. Woman's beauty has led many astray; it kindles a desire like a flame. *Sir 9:7-9*

Nor is this surprising:

Can a man hug fire to his breast without setting his clothes alight?   *Prov 6:27*

as much as to say "No!"

Because of this, the Apostle Paul, urges:

Keep away from fornication.   *1 Cor 6:18*

and Lot was told, as he fled from burning Sodom:

"Run for your life. Neither look behind you nor stop anywhere on the plain. Make for the hills if you would not be overwhelmed."   *Gen 19:17*

(2) Fire is also quenched by pouring on water. This means the pouring forth of tears:

Water quenches a blazing fire, almsgiving atones for sins.   *Sir 3:33*

What is that "almsgiving"? It is the almsgiving of compassion. Each one should first have compassion with himself and then with others; he should weep first for his own faults and then for those of others. Gregory comments that "the penitent person ought to wash himself daily in tears."[4] This is what the Psalmist did:

I am worn out with groaning, every night I drench my pillow and soak my bed with tears.   *Ps 6:6*

Indeed, one should do this because of his own sins and those of others:

Up, cry out in the nighttime, in the early hours of darkness; pour your heart out like water before Yahweh.

                    Lam 2:19

Each person, then, ought to quench this fire in himself.
It is enkindled daily:

There is no virtuous man on earth who, doing good, is
ever free from sin.   *Eccles 7:21*

If we say we have no sin in us, we are deceiving ourselves and refusing to admit the truth.   *1 Jn 1:8*

(3) Finally, fire is quenched by blasts of wind. This, indeed, refers to the final evaluation when the Lord, with a
strong blast, will quench through his anger those who are
unwilling to quench in themselves their guilt by repentance:

The wicked man's light must certainly be put out, his
brilliant flame cease to shine.   *Job 18:5*

At that moment his "light must certainly be put out"
when that pronouncement is made:

Bind him hand and feet and throw him out into the dark!
                                                        Mt 22:13

Then all his delight will perish and

the crime will be ground up along with the criminal.
                                                        *Sir 27:3

One shudders violently at the very thought of that
"quenching" which occurs through the wind of divine in-
dignation! Consequently, be careful of the blasts of devilish
subtlety as Job says of Behemoth:

From his mouth come fiery torches, sparks of fire fly
out of it. His nostrils belch smoke like a caldron boiling on
the fire. His breath could kindle coals, so hot a flame
issues from his mouth.   *Job 41:10-12*

Therefore his subtlety must be avoided. If, however, anyone has yielded to his suggestions in any way, the sensible
action is to hasten to the "streams of water," i.e., streams
of tears:

As a doe longs [driven by the heat] for running streams,
so longs my soul for you, my God.   *Ps 42:1*

First, however, it is proper to drag away those logs,
i.e., the opportunities for sin, so that the cause for guilt
is not renewed. Second, remember that the more this earthly

fire is quenched, the more the heavenly fire is enkindled which the Lord today "sent down from on high" upon the Apostles. May the Son of God who is blessed for all ages send this fire down upon each one of us.

III. The third fire is the fire of repentance which in some way is "from the depths" and in some way is "from on high." It comes from the depths according to what guilt deserves but from on high because of the decision of Divine Justice. Furthermore, this fire has two different aspects: (a) the fire of present problems, and (b) the fire of eternal condemnation. The first must be endured: the second, prevented.

(a) The fire of present problems should be endured for three reasons:

(1) This fire scrubs us clean:

Yes, he is coming, says Yahweh Sabaoth. Who will be able to resist the day of his coming? Who will remain standing when he appears? For he is like the refiner's fire and the fullers' alkaki. He will take his seat as refiner and purifier; he will purify the sons of Levi. *Mal 3:2-3*

i.e., through the sending of problems through which the "sons of Levi," i.e., individuals committed to God, are purified but, contrariwise, the uncommitted are destroyed:

The bellows blast away to make the fire burn away the lead. In vain: the smelter does his work, but the dress is not purged out. *Jer 6:29*

Nature is destroyed but wickedness grows and increases.

(2) This fire must be endured because it proves us serviceable:

He knows of every step I take. He has tested me like gold which is refined in the fire. **Job 23:10*

Consequently he proves us and favors us because he himself "knows of my steps," i.e., the knowledge of approval. He does not prove us for his own knowledge but that each person may be known to himself in good qualities both towards himself and his neighbor. Concerning such "proving" by which a person is proven in himself through problems:

You probe my heart, examine me at night, you test me yet find nothing, no murmuring from me. *Ps 17:3*

i.e. murmurings from an impatient heart.

Concerning the "proving" of conversation with one's neighbor:

My son, if you aspire to serve the Lord, prepare yourself for an ordeal . . . since gold is tested in the fire, and chosen men in the furnace of humiliation. *Sir 2:1, 5*

The method is thus described:

These sufferings bring patience, as we know, and patience brings perseverance, and perseverance brings hope, and this hope is not deceptive. *Rom 5:3-5*

(3) The fire of present problems should be endured because it toughens us. Just as actual fire in the kiln toughens the earthenware vessels, but does not destroy them, so, too, the fire of problems toughens spiritual vessels:

Should you walk through fire, you will not be scorched and the flames will not burn you. For I am Yahweh, your God. *Is 43:2*

This happens if you have been a follower of God:

since the arms of the wicked are doomed to break, and Yahweh will uphold the virtuous. *Ps 37:17*

Consequently,

even in the middle of the fire I was not burned. *Sir 51:6*

This is not surprising. Just as problems sting from the outside, so divine encouragement soothes from the inside:

Indeed, as the sufferings of Christ overflow to us, so, through Christ, does our consolation overflow. *2 Cor 1:5*

Those vessels which lack this divine encouragement are not "fired" but broken because of their impatience:

But godless men are all like desert thorns, for these are never gathered by hand: no one touches them unless with iron or the shaft of a spear, and then they are burnt in the fire. *2 Sam 23:6-7*

because they do not know how to endure that fire. In such

fire, then, were destroyed those slaves of the king of Israel who wanted to seize Elijah:

If I am a man of God, let fire come down from heaven and destroy both you and your fifty men.   *2 Kings 1:10*

This did happen as is related in the same place in Scripture.

(b) The fire of eternal condemnation, because of its complex dreadfulness, should be dreaded and prevented:

(1) It is unquenchable:

He will gather his wheat into the barn; but the chaff he will burn in a fire that will never go out.   *Mt 3:12*

This "chaff" are those sinners who have a meager amount of grace and are deficient in good actions. They will be burnt "in that fire that never goes out" when they are cast down into the depths:

Their worm will not die nor their fire go out.   *Is 66:24*

The reason for this is that it is divine not human power than enkindles it:

For in Topheth there has been prepared beforehand, yes, made ready for Molech, a pit deep and wide, with straw and wood in plenty. The breath of Yahweh, like a stream of brimstone, will set fire to it.   *Is 30:33*

Since he has sinned against the justice of God, he will be punished for eternity in those fiery depths which have been "prepared beforehand," i.e., from the beginning:

Go away from me, with your curse upon you, to the eternal fire prepared for the devil and his angels.   *Mt 25:41*

(2) This fire should be dreaded because it is unbearable with its harshness:

May red-hot embers rain down on them, may they be flung into the abyss for good.   *Ps 140:10*

They will be "flung into the abyss for good" where so much afflicts them that they cannot endure it. Nor is this surprising:

He rains coals of fire and brimstone on the wicked, he serves them scorching wind as their cup-portion.   **Ps 11:6*

Into this fire sinners will be thrust:

Sinners in Zion are struck with horror and fear seizes on the godless. Which of you can live with this devouring fire? Which of you can exist in everlasting flames? *Is 33:14*

It is as though he says "No one!"
Therefore Paul cautions:

It is a dreadful thing to fall into the hands of the living God. *Heb 10:31*

For our God is a consuming fire. *Heb 12:29*

(3) This fire should be dreaded because it is unavoidable. No one will be able to flee:

Yes, a fire has blazed from my anger, it will burn to the depths of Sheol; it will devour the earth and all its produce, it will set fire to the foundations of the mountains. *Deut 32:22*

No one, be he unimportant or important, will be able to escape the fire of divine fury:

A fire precedes him as he goes, devouring all enemies around him. *Ps 97:3*

Consequently, in no way can anyone escape — neither from outside nor within:

You will make them like a blazing furnace, the day that you appear, Yahweh will engulf them in his anger and fire will devour them. *Ps 21:9*

Shudder at the thought of being thrust headlong into such fire!

Whoever does not wish to be thrust down like this must be very humble:

Be very humble since the punishment for the godless is fire and worms. *Sir 7:19*

Humbleness, indeed, is the spirit which frees one from the fire of gehenna and obtains that fire which is "sent from on high." Augustine insists that "we are more filled with love in proportion as we are healed of the cancer of pride." [5] The basis, then, of complete spiritual health is sincere humbleness.

May the Lord grant this to us. . . .

NOTES

(1) Bonaventure, *op. cit.*, IX, pp. 341 - 345: In Pentecoste - sermo 9. This homily is also found in the editio minor, V, pp. 360 - 368.

(2) Bernard, *Epist.* III, n. 3.

(3) Gregory, *In Evang.* II, hom. 30, n. 2.

(4) Gregory, *Super Cant.*, c. 4, n. 9.

(5) Augustine, *De. Trin.*, VIII, c. 8, n. 12.

Christ "sent" Francis a "purple robe," the marks of the passion, when he impressed on him the stigmata of his own wounds. Thus the words of the apostle Paul are appropriate to Francis: "The marks on my body are those of Jesus" (Gal 6:17). — St. Bonaventure, *Homilies*.

My Friend

〰〰〰〰〰〰〰〰〰〰〰〰〰〰〰〰〰〰〰〰〰〰〰〰〰〰

MY FRIEND, MOVE UP HIGHER!   *Lk 14:10*

These are the words of the Lord who invites us to humility. Just before, the Lord had said:

When someone invites you to a wedding-feast . . . make your way to the lowest place and sit there.

Blessed Francis, invited to the wedding-feast of Jesus Christ, sat in the lowest place: he had chosen a very humble garb when he began the Order of Friars Minor. He named them simply and completely "Friars Minor" rather than by some special title. Christ could easily say to him, "My friend, move up higher!" In this is fulfilled the Psalmist's word:

He raises the poor from the dust; he lifts the needy from the dunghill to give them a place with princes, with the princes of his people.   *Ps 113:7-8*

However, in these words, three facets should be considered: (1) grace in the present life—"my friend"; (2) the passing from this life—"move up"; (3) glory in the future life—"higher".

(1) "My friend":

In each generation she passes into holy souls, she makes them friends of God and prophets; for God loves only the man who lives with Wisdom.   *Wis 7:27*

Translator's Note: Bonaventure preached this homily[1] for the commemoration of the dedication of the Basilica of St. Francis at Assisi. This feast is now celebrated on May 24. The homily is a beautiful and simple expression of that intimacy or friendship-with-the-Lord felt and acted upon by Francis — and open to anyone of us.

Readily could Christ call Francis "friend" because, in fact, he was, even in this life, his friend: (a) loyal in any enterprise through his real humility; (b) agreeable in any plan through his soundness of heart; (c) reliable in the barracks because of his calm thinking; (d) similar in marks of honor from the visible moulding of the cross.

(a) A faithful friend is something beyond price, there is no measuring his worth.   *Sir 6:15*

Indeed, Francis was "loyal in any enterprise" because he became involved neither in deceit nor negligence. Gregory comments that "two things must be guarded against in the works of the Lord—deceit and negligence. Too much love of self engenders deceit; too little love of others brings on negligence."[2] Francis, however, was harsh with himself but very kind to others. Thus he avoided both faults and, consequently, was "loyal." He was also "loyal" because he so completely obeyed the Lord's commands; he took to himself nothing of the Lord's gifts. You are indeed a faithful servant of the Lord if, from those possessions of the Lord which are transferred through you, even though they are not from you, nothing has stuck to your fingers.

(b) Yahweh loves the pure in heart, friend to the king is the man of gracious speech.   *Prov 22:11*

Two things foster this soundness of heart: (1) repentance in freely-accepted pain, and (2) endurance in distress imposed by others. These are the scouring-pads which cleanse the spirit—first through water; second, through fire:

You tested us, God, you refined us like silver, you let us fall into the net, you laid heavy burdens on our backs, you let people drive over our heads; but now the ordeal by fire and water is over, and you allow us once more to draw breath.   *Ps 66:10-12*

Just as it is impossible to cleanse a stained shirt unless it goes to the cleaners, so too the spirit unless it goes through the cleansing-agents of repentance and endurance. Since:

a friend is a friend for all times   *Prov 17:17*

one always ought ro have this soundness of heart:

If a man washes after touching a corpse, and then touches it again, what is the good of his washing? Just so with a man who fasts for his sins and then goes off and commits them again. Who will listen to his prayers? What is the good of his self-abasement? *Sir 24:30-31*

(c) The bridegroom's friend, who stands there and listens, is glad when he hears the bridegroom's voice. *Jn 3:29*

The "friend," Francis, of the "bridegroom," Christ, "heard his voice" because it was very familiar to him from calm contemplation. Therefore, it can be said of him:

Yahweh would speak with Moses face to face, as a man speaks with his friend. *Ex 33:11*

Moses, rescued from the waters, Francis from the waves of worldly concerns whom the Lord sent with the rod of the Cross to lead the people from the Egypt of wickedness into the desert of sanctity in the Friars Minor (cf. Ex 2:5, 2:10).

(d) Alexander sent Jonathan a purple robe and a golden crown and he said, "You are to study our interests and maintain friendly relations with us . . . " *1 Mac 10:20

Christ "sent" Francis a "purple robe"—the marks of his passion when he impressed on him the stigmata of his own wounds. Thus the words of the apostle Paul are appropriate to Francis:

the marks on my body are those of Jesus. *Gal 6:17*

Francis, then, was the friend of Christ—loyal in any enterprise—agreeable in any plan—reliable in the barracks—similar in marks of honor.

(2) "Move up," therefore, is said to such a person. Move up through me, following me, towards me, because of me. Move up:

(a) through me—affectionately imploring through prayer; (b) following me—deliberately copying in conversation; (c) towards me—clearly observing in contemplation; (d) because of me—at the last, apprehending in glory.

(a) The first is pre-figured in Genesis:

Jacob saw a ladder, standing on the ground with its top reaching to heaven; and there were angels of God going up it and coming down.   *Gen 28:12

Christ is the "ladder"—in his humanity "standing on the ground"; in his divinity "reaching to heaven." By this ladder Francis ascended:

What is this coming up from the desert (of repentance) like a column of smoke, breathing of myrrh (through sorrow) and frankincense (through love) and every perfume (a gathering of virtues) the merchant knows.   Song 3:6

(b) The second is pre-figured in Samuel:

Jonathan climbed up, hands and feet, with his armor-bearer behind him.   1 Sam 14:13

For "Jonathan" substitute "Christ"; "hands and feet," the crucifixion; his "armor-bearer" is Francis who carried his arms, i.e., the stigmata.

(c) The third is pre-figured where the Lord is reported to have said to Moses:

Climb the mountain . . . and view the land which I am giving the sons of Israel.   *Deut 32:49

The "mountain" is Christ about whom it is said:

The stone broken away from the mountain, untouched by any hand . . . grew into a great mountain filling the whole earth.   *Dan 2:34-36

(d) The fourth is pre-figured in the Song of Songs:

I will climb the palm tree . . . I will seize its cluster of dates.   Song 7:8

The palm is the tree whose trunk is the lower part if narrow but, higher up, wider. Christ, in his humanity was:

a little less than the angels;   *Ps 8:5

in his divinity, Creator and Lord of angels and of all. The fruit of this tree consists in gazing upon it and in enjoying it. Augustine said[3] "gazing upon it is the whole reward."

And eternal life is this: to know you, the only true God, and Jesus Christ whom you have sent.   Jn 17:3

NOTES

(1) Bonaventure, *op. cit.*, IX, pp. 534 - 535: De Translatione S. Francisci.

(2) Gregory, *Moral.* IX, c. 34, n. 53.

(3) Augustine, *Expositio in Ps.* 90, 13.

Love's Command

JESUS SAID, "YOU MUST LOVE THE LORD YOUR GOD WITH ALL YOUR heart, with all your soul, and with all your mind."

Mt 22:37; Deut 6:5

[Subtheme]: For thus Yahweh speaks to me: "From where I am, I gaze untroubled, like the clearness of midday heat, like a dewy mist in the midst of harvest." *Is 18:4*

In the subtheme, divine wisdom is described as fiery, bright, cool, and fruitful: "fiery," as I interpret it, in contrast to lukewarm carelessness; "bright" against shadowy unawareness; "cool" in contrast to lust's heats; and "fruitful" in contrast to greed's dryness. The meaning of "fiery" in contrast to lukewarm carelessness is indicated in the phrase "midday heat": light at midday has greater intensity. The meaning of "bright" against shadowy unawareness is described by the word "clearness." "Cool" in contrast to lust's heats is intended by the phrase "a dewy mist" and "fruitful" in contrast to greed's dryness is shown in the final phrase "in the midst of harvest."

First of all, since it is our joint effort to drink something from the deep depth of Divine Wisdom—setting it forth drop by drop—let us humbly beg our merciful Source-giver that, in his gentle concern, during our dialogue, he may free us

---

Translator's Note: Fr. Bougerol has identified this homily [1] as given by Bonaventure at Paris on October 1, 1251, the "17th Sunday after Pentecost." It is one of the fifty "sermones de Tempore" which Bonaventure himself gathered together and published during his first years of teaching at the University. The full expansion of the homily-form is seen here as the subtheme leads into prayer before the chosen text is subdivided and carefully elaborated. The recurring triplets in the subdivisions reinforce a Trinitarian theme and emphasize "love" in all its totality and richness.

from lukewarm carelessness, shadowy unawareness, lust's heats, and greed's dryness. Then, indeed, we may become "fiery, bright, cool, and fruitful" in these discussions relating to His praise and glory.

You must love the Lord your God . . . .

It is characteristic of great generosity to share oneself, lawfully, with the hostile and unfriendly. Our Lord, like a good teacher, wished to share his teaching of truth even with the spiteful Jews who deceitfully questioned him. To their inquiry concerning practicality, although it came from their spiteful spirit, he responded in truth: "You must love the Lord your God. . . . ." In these words, in a tactful yet marvelous way, he carefully involved the "whole person" in responding with all his capacities to love God—helped by the threefold virtues of faith, hope, and love. First, with the greatest love, he directs deep desire by commanding the action of love. Second, with the greatest concern, he lessens angry reactions by introducing a focus on Divinity. Third, with the greatest understanding, he gives light to probing reason by explaining the subtleties of truth from the vantage point of the highest intelligible. The first relates to love; the second, to hope; the third, to faith.

1. He commands the prized action of love by directing deep desire when he says "You must love." That action of love is lured out by the power of desire.

2. He introduces that important focus on Divinity thereby lessening angry reactions, when he says "the Lord your God." God, first and most importantly, is the focus of love. Therefore the love of God is

the first and greatest commandment. *Mt 22:39*

We should not love our neighbor nor any other human being except because of God or in God by reason of this divine image and likeness. This is why

the second [commandment] resembles it. *Mt 22:39*

If, however, anyone loves another in any way other than because of God or in God—for example because of family relationships, or human attraction, or some convenience—this is a natural act and not the result of the essence of love.

3. He clarifies the practical side of truth by making its subtleties explicit when he says, "with all your heart, with all your soul, and with all your mind."

I. "You must love." Here he commands an action of love. That action of loving, by reason of the essence of love, is of incomparable importance, usefulness, and value. This is the first and most important command of the Law and is even called "the greatest." There are three reasons for this: (a) regarding the commands, love has prime value in "being"; (b) regarding the virtues, it has greater worth in "earning"; (c) regarding activities, it offers the pleasurable acceptance of "reward." In this way the Lord gives commands a forceful efficiency; he assigns to virtues the appearance of beauty; he grants to activity a measure of repayment. O God-fashioning virtue! in which all commands are deeply-rooted, through which other virtues are shaped and rewarded, and according to which all activities are accepted!

(a) That command "to love," then, in relation to other commands has the prime value in "being." Love, therefore, gives commands their forceful efficiency. Of the text:

This is my commandment: love one another as I have loved you.   *Jn 15:2*

Gregory says, "Why is it that the Lord urges us concerning love as though about some very special mandate—unless it is that all commands are many and one? Many in their diversity of activity; one in their being rooted in love."[2]

It is the same reason that we find in today's Gospel:

On these two commandments hang the whole Law, and the Prophets also.   *Mt 22:40*

They provide a firm, strong foundation to lead us to the love of God and of our neighbor. Understanding this, Paul wrote:

rooted in love and built on love, you will with all the saints have strength to grasp the breadth and the length, the height and the depth; until, knowing the love of Christ, which is beyond all knowing, you are filled with the utter fullness of God.   **Eph 3:18-19*

Wretched fools who lack this foundation! Whatever they build, collapses completely in ruins. Consequently, actions done without love never flourish; they are without root. Gregory, in the same homily, says, "No branch has any greenness unless it stays in the root of love."

(b) That command "to love," in relation to other virtues, has greater worth in "earning." Love, therefore, shapes the other virtues:

The greatest of these is love.   *1 Cor 13:13*

Paul, in speaking about all the virtues, social as well as spiritual, concludes from both negative and positive reasoning that love is the greatest. If love is present, everything is done meritoriously; without love nothing is useful for salvation. Therefore, love alone provides the formula for "earning"; other virtues are "formula-less" without love. Just as colors lose their clarity and beauty as the light fades but recover them as the light increases, so too virtues when love is missing:

But anyone who loves his brother is living in the light and need not be afraid of stumbling; unlike the man who hates his brother and is in the darkness, not knowing where he is going, because it is too dark to see.   *1 Jn 2:10-11*

And so Augustine says, "Love and do what you wish!"[3]

(c) That command "to love," in relation to activities, offers pleasurable acceptance of "reward." Thus he grants to activity a measure of repayment. In proportion as we love in this life, we will be given shares in the glory of heaven. Where there is more love, there will be a closer approach to God. The greatness of our future reward depends not on exterior actions but on interior love. This is why martyrdom, which is of the greatest reward of all the actions which a person performs, is said to be an activity of greater love:

A man can have no greater love than to lay down his life for his friends.   *Jn 15:13*

Paul explains:

All the commandments . . . are summed up in this single

command, "You must love your neighbor as yourself." Love
is the one thing that cannot hurt your neighbor; that is why
it is the answer to every one of the commandments.

Rom 13:9-10

In other words, if a person is weak and remiss in fulfilling
other commandments, he can regain strength through love
which is generous and complete. Gregory comments, "No
wonder, since love is one and the same; if it has really
filled a person, love encourages him to countless actions in
many ways."[4]   If however a person is lacking in love, he
cannot replace it by other virtues:

A loving character cannot be weighed on the scales.

*Sir 26:20

II. "the Lord your God"—Thus he introduces that important focus on Divinity, i.e., on the Trinity. These three
words, "Lord your God," are not apart from the mystery of
the Trinity; through them is manifested a trinity of divine
persons who confer upon us three tremendous blessings.
Through these we are drawn delightedly towards the love
of God: (a) "Lord"—because of the natural condition of being
in creation; (b) "God"—because of the gathering of many
graces in salvation; (c) "your"—because of the gift of himself, i.e., everlasting inheritance in glory. Therefore, speaking aptly, we are created through the Father's power;
saved through the Son's wisdom; glorified through the Holy
Spirit's compassion.

(a) "You must love the Lord" because of the natural condition of being in creation:

And now, Israel, what does Yahweh your God ask of you?
Only this: to fear Yahweh your God, to follow all his ways,
to love him, to serve Yahweh your God with all your heart
and all your soul.   *Deut 10:12-13*

Mankind is held and obliged to fear the Lord humbly, to
obey faithfully and to love fervently because of the blessings
which the Lord gave him in creation. At that time he made
mankind's "being" stamped with his own divine image.
Therefore he has the capability to fulfill these demands.
And so he has a right to demand these of us. When he

says, "Only this: to fear Yahweh your God," note the humble reverence and service which is required; "to follow all his ways" asks for faithful effort in obedience to his commands, i.e., "his ways"; "to love him" invites intense "one-ness" and good-will.

(b) "You must love God" because of the gathering of many graces in salvation:

You who love Yahweh, hate evil! Yahweh guards the soul of the devout, rescuing them from the clutches of the wicked.   *Ps 97:10*

"You who love God" by doing good through love, "hate evil" by turning from sin through reverence of God. Through this love and reverence for God, individuals are made holy and merit God's blessings of care and salvation. "He guards the souls of the devout" by gathering together many blessings. The service of good actions accompanies this guiding care. Angels minister to him; the heavens give him light in day so he can work and darkness at night for his rest and also useful changes of weather. God made the air that he might give mankind its useful warmth and that all kinds of birds might serve him. He made the waters to quench his thirst, cleanse dirt, and irrigate dry lands as well as giving a variety of fish for his nourishment. He made the earth to support him:

wine to make them cheerful, oil to make them happy and bread to make them strong.   *Ps 104:15*

The whole universe serves mankind because it was created for him. By reason of such great blessings, "you who love Yahweh" show it through your performance of good actions. At another time we will discuss ingratitude.

(c) "You must love the Lord your God" because of the gift of everlasting inheritance in glory:

I love the beauty of the house where you live, the place where your glory makes its home.   *Ps 26:8*

This "beauty" is nothing other than the divine brightness from which flash rays of divine splendor. These make the highest reaches of heaven into a home of beauty because of the brightness of divine splendor. It is the "place where your glory makes its home" because of this sharing in the glory of divinity. O how bright and attractive is that "beauty of your house," O God! With what attentive yearning do we love it! How happy and holy is that "place where your glory makes its home!" How hungrily we seek it! For there God shares himself more abundantly and joyfully with the blessed and is in-dwelling in them in glory!

III. "with all your heart, with all your soul, and with all your mind"—Here he explains the practical manner of truth. In a marvelous and indescribable way, our great teacher, Christ Jesus, taught how God should be loved by these words: (a) "heart," (b) "soul," and (c) "mind." A person cannot love God unless he is united to him; he cannot be united unless he knows him, "has" him, and holds him as far as his three human powers enable, i.e., understanding, desire, and memory. It is in these that mankind is, "in the image of God" according to Augustine. [5]

"To know" is an activity of the understanding; "to have" is one of desire; and "to hold" concerns memory. Therefore, necessarily, to love God requires the activity of all three of these powers together. This is indicated by "heart, soul, mind": understanding as a function of the heart; desire, of the soul; memory, of the mind. In this interpretation we are following Augustine. Consequently, God must be loved faithfully so that the understanding is not seduced by false errors. God must be loved totally so that desire is not attracted by worldly concerns. God must be loved endlessly so that memory is not broken by discontinuity. This explanation follows Augustine who expounds the passage in this way: [6]

"With all your heart, i.e., with understanding without error; with all your soul, i.e., with desire without contradictions; with all your mind, i.e., with memory without forgetfulness."

Thus divine love clarifies all we ought to believe; provides an unconcern with worldly delights; and motivates a constancy in good actions.

(a) "You must love the Lord your God with all your

heart", i.e., with the steadfast faith of understanding lest you be seduced by deceptions:

Listen, Israel: Yahweh our God is the only God. You shall love Yahweh your God with all your heart . . .   *Deut 6:4*

"Listen Israel"—believe firmly in your heart that there are no other gods. In no way can you imagine unequals to have any equality. "You shall love the Lord your God with all your heart" by efficiently proving in your actions that you admit no contrary interests. Nothing else ought to bind our heart in love except to him who ought to be loved by our whole heart. When we love anyone or anything above God or beyond God, we love worthlessly. Just as the understanding errs in knowing, so desire errs in loving.

(b) "You must love the Lord. your God with all your soul," i.e., with such a totality of desire that you are not enticed by others' flattery:

My spirit melted when my Beloved spoke to me.
                                                    Song 5:6

Indeed, the "spirit melts" from the honey-sweet, gentle whisper of God just as

wax melts when near the fire   *Ps 68:2*

when

at the thought of him, if flared up with the fire of divine love   *Ps 39:3*

and then is released into a depth of prayerfulness and spiritual intensity—just as ice is melted by the heat of a material fire. When one's spirit is most deeply touched with yearning and love, it completely withdraws into itself in order not to be distracted by the rain-clouds of worldly cares. Immersed by the pouring out of divine love, the whole spirit is in flames.

(c) "You must love the Lord your God with all your mind" —i.e. with the earnest zeal of love lest you be deterred by daily tasks:

Yahweh said, "If only their mind were always so, set on the fear of me and the keeping of my commandments.
                                                    Deut 5:29

See how the Lord shows his generous concern for us! He desires that through filial fear of him we may constantly, endlessly, and ever increasingly fulfill his commands so that there be fulfilled in us that:

A friend is a friend at all times. *Prov 17:17*

Divine love, by reason of its constancy, ought to be similar to death and hell: what they once take is never let go:

Love is strong as Death, jealousy relentless as Sheol. The flash of it is a flash of fire, a flame of Yahweh himself. Love no flood can quench, no torrents drown.

Song 8:6-7

Let us, therefore, beseech . . . .

NOTES

(1) Bonaventure, *op. cit.*, IX, pp. 418 - 421: Dom. XVII post Pentecosten - sermo 1 cf. Bougerol, *op. cit.*, p. 147.
(2) Gregory, *Homil. in Evang.* II, 27, n. 1 super Ioan. 15, 12.
(3) Augustine, *In Epist. Ioan*, c. 4, tr. 7, n. 8.
(4) Gregory, *Moral.* X, c. 6, n. 9.
(5) Augustine, *De Trin.* X, c. 11, 12.
(6) Augustine, *Sermo* 108.

Such Love

HER MANY SINS HAVE BEEN FORGIVEN HER, FOR SHE HAS SHOWN GREAT
love.   *Lk 7:47*

First of all, let us ask . . . .

Dear friends in Christ Jesus: According to the tradition of
Sacred Scripture, when the world lost its wholeness, "woman" who had been created to help "man" became, in an
important way, a stumbling-block for him. She was involved
in the loss of his integrity for, through her, man stumbled
into sin; she was also involved in his delay to repent for
he used her as the motive to counter his own blame. Both
were important failures. To right the balance, in the re-
building of the world, "woman" is also presented to us—
first, as a mirror of integrity and second, as a model for
repentance. Our mirror of integrity is the glorious Virgin
Mary, Mother of Christ; our model for repentance is Mary
Magdalene, who loved Christ so deeply. It is characteristic
of divine wisdom that, since these two dimensions could not
be joined in one individual, both enjoyed the same name.
Mary Magdalene, then, is shown us as our model for repentance. For this reason, today's Gospel says "Her many
sins have been forgiven her, because she has shown such
great love."

These words, chosen for her praise and our encouragement,
clarify two aspects: (1) the constant state of love, i.e.,

Translator's Note: This homily [1] was preached by Bonaventure on the feast
of Mary Magdalene, July 22. There is a special warmth and tenderness filling these words on that deep love which Magdalene showed in her actions
and her words. Here, too, the four-fold subdivisions declare the depth of
that reality of love to which we are all invited.

"since she has loved much," and (2) the result of such love, i.e., "her many sins are forgiven her."

Indeed, she seems to have loved Christ more than any of the others. In this love we can consider four facets: (a) the beginnings of love, (b) the manner of love, (c) the marks of love, and (d) the enjoyments of love.

(a) First, I say, we ought to consider the beginnings of love. It seems from Scripture that Mary Magdalene began to love Christ deeply in a love that was four-faceted. For a person is moved to do something for various reasons, e.g., to avoid misfortune, to gain profit, to maintain integrity, to find peace.

A person is moved to do something to avoid misfortune when he sees that something is advantageous. Mary Magdalene, then, to avoid the misfortunes of death, began to love:

If you refuse to love, you must remain dead.   *1 Jn 3:14*

Natural life is broken when the unity of body and spirit is broken. Christ is the everlasting life of the spirit; love is the bond by which he is united to our spirit. Whenever that bond is broken, death comes to the spirit. In order to avoid such a misfortune, she began to love Christ deeply. This certainly she had learned from her Teacher. Mary had heard that young man asking the Lord what he should do

to possess eternal life.   *Mt 19:16*

Jesus replied:

Keep the commandments!   *Mt 19:16*

Afterwards he taught about the love of God and of neighbor and then said:

Do this and life is yours!   *Lk 10:28*

When she heard this, she began to love ever more deeply.

A person is moved to do something to gain profit. But what is the "profit" of love? Certainly, the eternal kingdom! Therefore, everyone should strive to come to this love. When the spirit loves Christ very deeply, it becomes the bride of Christ and Christ is

Lord of lords and King of kings.   *Rev 17:14*

Thus it is appropriate that the spirit become queen:

If then . . . you delight in throne and sceptre, honor Wisdom, thus to reign forever.   *Wis 6:22*

Think about all that the Bridegroom wishes his bride to have! He wants her skin to be fresh and glowing, for her to be beautifully gowned, and completely united to him. Well, love cleanses the pores of sin just as blazing fire cleanses grime and rust from iron. Therefore, "her many sins have been forgiven her, for she has shown great love."

Love covers over many a sin.   *1 Pet 4:8*

The spirit should be "beautifully· gowned" and love is that beauty of spirit which turns one to God. The spirit, like an angel, must be transformed into whatever it gazes towards—just as a mirror reflects whatever likeness approaches it. Likewise, it is right and fitting that the spirit be completely united to Christ Jesus:

You are wholly beautiful, my love, and without a blemish.
      Song 4:7

The spirit, beautiful in its purity, replies, "that beauty is not mine but yours for you are wholly beautiful and without a blemish." It is as though the spirit says, "Since the moment I turned towards you and became united to you, necessarily, your beauty and likeness make me beautiful." Let us all, then, love in this way.

A person is moved to do something to maintain integrity. For this reason, too, Mary Magdalene was moved to love Christ. There is nothing sweeter nor more appropriate than Christ-loving. There is no comparison to his love. He says:

I love those who love me, those who seek me eagerly shall find me.   *Prov 8:17*

David was chided because he had hatred for those who loved him (cf. 2 Sam. 19:6-8). It is unnatural for a person not to love someone who loves him. Since Christ

loved us first,   **1 Jn 4:10*

God the Father sent his Son . . . to redeem us.   **Gal 4:4*

Let us say nothing about the goods of nature bestowed upon us and the everlasting joys promised to us and the universe subject to us. Let us just reflect that "he sent his son"—and fully saved us! We shall see that we are bound to love him. Why, then, do you not give him your heart? Certainly, "Oh Israel, you are acting unjustly" (cf Gen 16:5). See what God wants:

that you love Yahweh, your God, with all your heart . . . and follow his ways.   *Deut 30:6, 16

A person is moved to do something to find peace. Nothing, however, abounds more in peace and pleasure than to love God. If someone should say, "Look! Here is some honey that is so sweet one drop would sweeten the whole ocean! And once you taste a drop of this honey, everything else will taste bitter!" Well—such honey would, indeed, be very sweet. Yet there is such sweetness in Divine Love and it transforms all bitterness and all everyday problems into sweetness. Likewise, once a person has tasted this sweetness, everything else tastes bitter. As Bernard says, "When one has tasked of the spirit, all flesh becomes tasteless."[2] Mary Magdalene had tasted this sweetness and wanted to taste nothing else. Indeed she even disregarded the angels and turned away from them in order to go looking for Jesus (cf John 20, 12).

Christ foretold of this sweetness:

Approach me, you who desire me, and take your fill of my fruits, for memories of me are sweeter than honey, inheriting me is sweeter than the honeycomb.   Sir 24:26-27

and again:

Wine and music cheer the heart; better than either, the love of wisdom.   Sir 40:20

This concludes our consideration of the beginnings of love.

(b) Now, let us consider the manner of love. Bernard wishes that "the measure of loving God be without measure."[3] I believe, however, that a four-termed covenant is required for a person to love rightly, i.e., honestly, uniquely, glowingly, and ceaselessly.

The first—honestly—demands that there be no other attraction, no insincerity; nay, rather that such great love blaze in the heart as one shows in exterior signs:

These who are faithful will live with him in love.   *Wis 3:9*

One who neglects gain because of a friend, is a just man.   **Prov 12:26*

It should not be a deceiving love which is only an empty embrace.

The second—uniquely—requires that nothing be loved above nor except Him; and that no other love be mixed with His. Love is a powerful mistress and if a person should have a heart tenfold larger than he has he would wish to fill himself totally here:

The heart knows its own good best nor can a stranger share its joy.   *Prov 14:10*

Because of this, Moses said:

Listen Israel, Yahweh our God is the one Yahweh. You shall love Yahweh, your God, with all your heart, with all your soul, with all your strength.   *Deut 6:5*

The Song of Songs says:

I am my Beloved's and my Beloved is mine.   *Song 6:2*

As though to say, "I am not going out after the adulterers of the world."

Third, we ought to love glowingly. This glowing heat is brought to bear on so great a burning desire that the spirit springs forth beyond its limits. Just as a splashing fountain goes out beyond itself, so the spirit, when it loves glowingly, goes beyond itself and wishes to approach what is beyond human strength:

For love is strong as Death, jealousy relentless as Sheol. The flash of it is a flash of fire, a flame of Yahweh himself.
                                                    Song 8:6

Mary Magdalene, because she loved so glowingly, wished to go beyond what strength would allow:

She went to the tomb   **Jn 20:1*

which the men did not dare to do. She offered to carry the

body of Jesus herself:

If you have taken him away, tell me where you have put him, and I will go and remove him.   *Jn 20:15*

Likewise, we must love ceaselessly—following the example of Christ:

He had always loved those who were his in the world, but now he showed how perfect his love was.   *Jn 13:1*

The reward for love is very great—life eternal. This ought to move us to love greatly:

To win Rachel, therefore, Jacob worked seven years, and they seemed to him like a few days because he loved her so much.   *Gen 29:20*

A friend is a friend for all times.   **Prov 17:17*

Somewhere else it is said, "He who abandons love before death should not be considered a friend." Here love is like a fire—but there it will be like a furnace! So much, then, concerning the origin and manner of love.

(c) Now, about the marks of love. True love has four signs: it shakes out inactivity; forces fear aside; shows no embarrassment; and does not harbor memory of suffering. Mary Magdalene was the woman who most perfectly loved Jesus. This love allowed her no idleness as we know from the accounts in Scripture of her activities during the public ministry of Christ, at the time of his death and afterwards. While Christ was living, she went up with him to Galilee and used her own resources to assist him. She followed him at the time of his death; she also came to the tomb. She embodies the text:

On my bed at night, I sought him whom my heart loves. I sought but did not find him. So I will rise and go through the City; in the streets and the squares, I will seek him whom my heart loves.   *Song 3:1-2*

But wretched man sleeps in his bed; he ought to get up with Mary and seek Christ!

Scarcely had I passed them than I found him whom my heart loves. I held him fast, nor would I let him go. . . .
                                              Song 3:4

She went first to Peter, then to John, first wept, then prayed, then went to the tomb and after a while she encountered Jesus.

Her love forced fear aside. She did not fear harm while she looked for Jesus:

If you have taken him away, tell me where you have put him and I will go and remove him.   *Jn 20:15*

Joseph of Arimathaea was a soldier and a friend of Pilate. Nevertheless, without Pilate's permission, he did not dare to remove the body of Christ. But she did not even ask for darkness: no! openly, in front of everyone, she wished to carry his body and she went to the tomb:

In love there can be no fear, for fear is driven out by perfect love.   *1 Jn 4:18*

But some men are so afraid for their own skins that they do not dare to move towards repentance!

Mary's love did not embarrass her. The Gospel relates that this mere woman entered among the dinner guests (cf. Lk 7:36-38), poured tears instead of using the usual basin of water, and in acknowledging her sinfulness was not embarrassed amongst those banquet-guests!"[4] Some people not only are too embarrassed to repent but are even uncomfortable in being called "good men." Certainly they ought to work to be what they appear. That woman, like one possessed, kept running back and forth:

Have you seen him whom my heart loves?   *Song 3:3*

And note: these were not just words in her mouth but from her heart.

Love is perfect when a person does not feel its pain. Let us see if she qualified in this aspect. She certainly grieved greatly over Lazarus' death and remained sitting in her house. When Christ arrived, Martha said to her:

The Master is here and wants to see you.   *Jn 11:28*

And then she did not feel grief over her brother's death, rather she complained of Christ's absence:

Lord, if you had been here, my brother would not have died.   *Jn 11:32*

As if to say, "I grieve over your absence." Paul, after mentioning various tribulations, says:

For your sake we are being massacred daily . . . These are the trials through which we triumph, by the power of him who loved us.   *Rom 8:36*

He is laughed at and does not notice it; he is beaten and does not feel it. If love has such results on earth—what will it be like in heaven!

May God bring us to such love! Amen.

NOTES

(1) Bonaventure, *op. cit.*, IX, pp. 558 - 560: De S. Maria Magdalena - sermo 2.
(2) Bernard, *Epist.* III, n. 3.
(3) Bernard, *De Deligendo Deo*, c. 1, n. 1.
(4) Gregory, *In Evang.* II, h. 33, n. 1.

Father, Son, and Holy Spirit

⚬⚬⚬⚬⚬⚬⚬⚬⚬⚬⚬⚬⚬⚬⚬⚬⚬⚬⚬⚬⚬⚬⚬⚬⚬⚬⚬⚬⚬⚬⚬⚬⚬⚬⚬⚬

THERE ARE THREE WITNESSES IN HEAVEN: THE FATHER, THE WORD, AND
and the Spirit, and these three are one. There are three witnesses on earth: the Spirit, the water, and the blood.

1 Jn 5:7-8

In these words, the certainty of the Trinity is stated for
us. There is a double set of guarantees: (1) evidence which
directs us upward and is manifested to us with truthfulness,
i.e., "There are three witnesses in heaven . . ."; (2) evidence which stabilizes our belief and accomplishes this in a
practical manner, i.e., "There are three witnesses on earth..."
Through the first set of guarantees we come to know the
mystery of the Trinity in philosophical exploration of truth;
through the second set, in the practical pursuit of virtue

The Blessed Trinity is the origin—producing, patterning,
and limiting or fulfilling everything:

All that exists comes from him; all is by him and for
him. To him be glory forever!   *Rom 11:36*

The Trinity is complete one-ness: therefore unlimited in
power because, as Aristotle points out, "all united virtue
is more infinite than multiplied virtue."[2] The Trinity is

Translator's Note: This long homily [1] parallels very closely the teaching on
the Trinity clarified in Bonaventure's *Disputed Questions on the Holy Trinity*
expounded at Paris in 1253. The homily is possibly from the same year. It
is, in fact, a compendium of teachings on the Trinity with reference to
"the authorities" and an explanation of variant interpretations. And yet,
because it is a homily, it has a compactness and clarity and immediacy
which differs from the more involved scholastic "Disputed Questions" and
brings the wonderful mystery of the Trinity into a somewhat more contain-
able grasp. The repeated triplets of attribute and subdivision reinforce
directly and subliminally the threeness of Trinity.

absolute truth: therefore outstanding in wisdom. The Trinity is total goodness: therefore fully complete and lasting. As Aristotle says, "Goodness and lastingness are the same "[3] Accordingly, there are twelve uniquely appropriate attributes like twelve "foundation stones" upon which is built the whole heavenly Jerusalem:

The city walls stood on twelve foundation stones.

Rev 21:14

That city has "twelve foundation stones" according to a four-fold tripleness. (1) The first series is One-ness, Equalness, and Jointness or Union. Alan de Lille, in his Rules of Theology, says [4] "In the Father is One-ness; in the Son, Equalness; in the Holy Spirit, the Jointness of One-ness and Equalness," i.e., Union. One-ness is assigned to the Father because, according to Augustine, "all multiplying starts from oneness."[5] Everything originates from the Father. Equalness is assigned to the Son because, in the order of nature, the origin of the Son comes before other productions. The Son is a production of the Father and it is fitting that he fathered a son equal to himself. Boethius says that "all inequality is recognized through equality."[6] In the Holy Spirit there is the Jointness of One-ness and Equalness because he is the love of the Father and the Son, i.e., the binding together of the two. (2) The second series is Power, Wisdom, and Goodness. Power is assigned to the Father, Wisdom to the Son, and Goodness to the Holy Spirit. (3) The third series is Grandeur, Integrity, Generosity —Grandeur in the Father, Generosity in the Son, and Integrity in the Holy Spirit. (4) The fourth series is Eternity, Beauty, and Joyfulness. Eternity is in the Father from whom everything comes just as from eternity come eternity and time, permanence and impermanence.

I. The mystery of the Blessed Trinity is seen in a four-fold way in the sky, according to different interpretations: (a) in footprint, (b) in likeness, (c) in sign, and (d) in personal mien. Accordingly, the vault of the heaven has 12 interpretations. The sky is called (1) the brightness of nature, (2) the engine of the universe, (3) the arrangement of beauty. In these three the Blessed Trinity shines forth in "footprint." The sky is called (4) recognizable energy, (5) mind anticipated by grace, (6) Battlefield-Church. In these the Trinity is recognized as in "likeness." The sky is also called (7) Sacred Scripture, (8) angelic hierarchy, (9) adopted human nature. In these the Trinity appears as in "sign." The sky is also called (10) eternal wisdom, (11) cause giving birth to everything, (12) the whole Trinity. In these, the Trinity appears in "personal mien."

(a) Let us consider, first, the Blessed Trinity manifest in the sky as in "footprint." This is done in three ways.

The first gives witness in the sky as (1) the brightness of nature:

Look up to the heaven and count the stars if you can.
Gen 15:5

The Lord wishes that his faithful look up at the sky to see there the radiance of the Creator, i.e., of the Blessed Trinity, in three aspects: Steadiness, Flowingness, Powerfulness. Steadiness witnesses to the Father; Flowingness to the Son; Powerfulness to the Holy Spirit. Nevertheless each one evidences the Trinity.

In Steadiness are discovered three, i.e., magnitude in the Father, beauty in the Son, a pouring forth of resources in the Holy Spirit. The magnitude of the sky gives witness to the Father:

Let them deduce from these how much mightier is he that has formed them, since through the grandeur and beauty of the creatures we may, by analogy, contemplate their Author.
Wis 13:4-5

The beauty of the sky gives witness to the Son:

Pride of the heights, shining vault, so, in a glorious spectacle, the sky appears. The sun, as he emerges, proclaims at his rising "A thing of wonder is the work of the Most High!" (cf. Sir 43:1).

The pouring forth of resources gives witness to the generosity of the Holy Spirit who pours forth an abundance of charismatic graces.

Likewise, in Flowingness are three considerations, i.e., light from which comes brightness and warmth which is the diffusion of light and brightness. The Father, then, is understood in light; the Son in brightness for he is begotten by the Father; warmth is the Holy Spirit proceeding from Father and Son.

Similarly, in its Powerfulness for earth's crops, there are three, i.e., beginning, charm, fruitfulness. Beginning is assigned to the Father, charm to the Son, and fruitfulness to the Holy Spirit.

The second "footprint" witness of the Blessed Trinity in the sky is as (2) the engine of the universe:

Alone I encircled the vault of the sky.   *Sir 24:8*

This is not said because it alone contains that bright, heavenly nature which is above, but because it contains that whole engine of the universe which is enclosed within the heavens:

Do I not fill heaven and earth? It is Yahweh who speaks.
Jer 23:24

In this, too, the Blessed Trinity gives witness in the sky by manifestations of "footprint." There are again three divisions: Creative Power, Being, and Activity. Certainly, Creative Power relates to the Father; Being, to the Son; Activity, to the Holy Spirit. But in each of these the Trinity shines forth.

In Creative Power there are three, i.e., the act of creating, of separating, and of beautifying. Creating, since it comes out of nothingness gives evidence of infinite power and so is attributed to the Father; separating, which is a function of wisdom, relates to the Son; beautifying, which is part of generosity, relates to the Holy Spirit.

In Being, indeed, there are similarly three, i.e., matter, shape, agreement. Matter, because of its capacity for all shapes and because, as Aristotle[7] says, it is "unborn," symbolizes the Father as the "cause" of all who created from nothing. Shape, through which is all activity, symbolizes the Son. Agreement, because of its union of matter and shape, symbolizes the Holy Spirit who is the union of Father and Son.

In Activity three things are involved, i.e., substance, power, action. Power's origin is in substance and from both substance and power proceeds action just as the Son's origin is in the Father and the Holy Spirit proceeds from both.

The third "footprint" witness of the Blessed Trinity in the sky is as (3) the arrangement of beauty. Indeed, the sky is the arrangement of beauty beyond other created bodies; all that is called beautiful is called "sky":

Who was it measured the waters with his fist and the heavens with an open hand? Who calculated with three fingers the dimensions of the heavens?   *Is 40:12*

By "waters" is understood the flux of matter in itself:

There was darkness over the deep, and God's spirit hovered over the waters.   *Gen 1:2*

This "measurement with a fist" indicated the imposition of forms which limits the flux of matter. It is called "measurement with a fist" because of the littleness of the flux compared to the greatness of Divinity. Or it is called this because the whole matrix of earth into which the waters were gathered is not, when compared to the immensity of Divinity, more than the size of a fist. The "heavens" are said to be measured "with an open hand" partly because they stabilized in their place and had "weight" which is a property of something being stabilized in a place and partly because they are stretched like a tent for our gaze:

You stretch the heavens out like a tent.   *Ps 104:2*

In this is noted the difference in measuring waters and heavens: the waters are measured "with a fist" but the heavens "with an open hand." The waters within the interior of the earth are held as in a clenched hand but the heavens seem to be spread out as when the fingers are extended. A fist is a hand pressed together: an open hand is stretched wide. "With three fingers" he is said to calculate the dimensions. These "three fingers" are interpreted in various ways, e.g.:

You ordered all things by measure, number, weight.

Wis 11:21

"Measure" then pertains to the Father, as a point of

reference for all limitation, because of the immensity of the
Creator. It is impossible for anything to be "unmeasured"
which had "non-being" and then "being." Therefore, no
creature is "unmeasured" nor everlasting but "measured."

"Number" looks to the Son because of his wisdom distinguishing and recognizing all things:

He decides the number of the stars and gives each of
them a name; our Lord is great, all-powerful, of infinite
understanding.   *Ps 147:4*

All distinguishing requires knowledge. Each single thing is
distinguished from another by number.

"Weight" looks to the Holy Spirit because of his generosity which completes all things—just as by weight each
single thing in its place is stabilized and completed.

To these three correspond another three which Augustine
mentions[8]: "manner, appearance, arrangement." In this,
then, manner equals measure; appearance equals number;
arrangement equals weight. Therefore, manner refers to the
Father; appearance, to the Son; arrangement, to the Holy
Spirit.

Or again, these "three fingers" are unit, truth, goodness.
Unity is the Father's; truth, the Son's; and goodness, the
Holy Spirit's.

These three interpretations of "fingers" are different because those from the Book of Wisdom relate to things according to Creative Power; Augustine's interpretation relates to Being; and the third provides a practical explanation.

To focus this towards ourselves, these "three fingers"
of God, by which he lifts the "weight" of our earthiness
upwards towards heaven, are the three hierarchical actions
which take place in our spirit, i.e., cleansing, enlightening,
fulfilling. Cleansing comes through faith:

God made no distinction between them and us, since he
purified their hearts by faith.   *Acts 15:9*

Enlightening, from prayerfulness; fulfilling, from the one-
ness of love.

The sky, therefore, in which the Trinity is manifest in

"footprint" is looked upon in various ways. Some people are delighted by the beauty even though they understand nothing. Some, indeed, delight in their understanding of what they read but do not apply it to their own life-style. Some are delighted by the beauty of the heavens and of creatures but do not understand the force of this—such are the non-Christians who remain deliberately indifferent. Some, indeed, are delighted by an understanding of the essence of the heavens and the stars but do not reverence the Creator in their understanding—rather, they trust in their own knowledge—such are the secular philosophers and scientists. Some, however, gaze at the heavens and there reverence the Trinity:

I look up at your heavens, made by your fingers, at the moon and the stars you set in place . . . Yahweh, our Lord, how great your name throughout the earth!   *Ps 8:3, 9*

This is the way that true Christians gaze upon the sky.

(b) Let us consider, second, the Blessed Trinity manifest in the sky as in "likeness." This, too, in three ways.

The sky is called (4) recognizable energy:

I had my tent in the heights, and my throne in a pillar of cloud.   *Sir 24:6*

This is subdivided in three, i.e., Power, Condition, Performance. Power witnesses in "likeness" to the Trinity in memory, understanding, and desire:

The Lord fashioned man from the earth . . . and made them in his own image.   *Sir 17:3*

The Gloss explains, "just as from the Father, the Son and from both, the Holy Spirit, so from memory is understanding and from both, desire." Condition is also represented as threefold, i.e., natural, intellectual, moral. Natural, which is the beginning and pours out the others, evidences the Father; intellectual, the Son; moral, the Holy Spirit. Performance is, likewise, of threefold division, i.e., discernment, knowledge, and love: what is reflected upon is known or understood and loved.

The second "likeness" witness to the Trinity is (5) heart anticipated by grace:

Yahweh is in his holy Temple, Yahweh whose throne is
in heaven.   *Ps 11:4*

As Augustine says, "the heart of the just man is the
abode of God."[9] This is the triple grace, i.e., grace which
sanctifies, grace which activates the theological virtues,
grace of universal presence.

Moreover, that grace which sanctifies is threefold and gives
a threefold witness, i.e., baptismal, penitential, and eternal.
Baptismal reflects the Father as Creator or Initiator; penitential, the Son as Redeemer; eternal, the Holy Spirit as
Fulfiller. That grace which activates the theological virtues,
likewise, is threefold, i.e., rooting in faith, uplifting in hope,
joining or spreading forth in love. The first applies to the
Father; the second, to the Son; the third, to the Holy Spirit.
The grace of universal presence, also, is threefold, i.e.,
reinforcing in virtues which strengthen the power to bring
forth actions which are virtuous and meritorious; preparing
with gifts which free the powers; fulfilling in joys which
leave the spirit complete in grace. The first is the Father;
the second, the Son; the third, the Holy Spirit.

The third "likeness" witness in the sky to the Trinity is
the bride of Christ, the (6) Battlefield-Church:

And now war broke out in heaven, when Michael with his
angels attacked the dragon. The dragon fought back with
his angels, but they were defeated and driven out of heaven.
                                                             Rev 12:7

That "war broke out" not in the heaven of the saints
because the devil never returned there after he was once
cast forth. However, in our church on earth there arise
many battles. In this "heaven," then, witness is given three
ways, i.e., authority, status, life-style. Authority is threefold,
i.e., that of the patriarchs, of the prophets, of the apostles.
The first belongs to the power-giving Father; the second, to
the truth-speaking Son; the third, to the sanctifying Holy
Spirit. Indeed, the prophets descend from the patriarchs
and the apostles from both just as the Son from the Father
and the Holy Spirit from both. Status is threefold, i.e.,
that of the laity which comes from natural birth and evi-

dences the Father, the Creator; that of the clergy which comes through the Sacraments of the Church and evidences the Son; that of the religious which evidences the Holy Spirit, the sanctifier. Life-style, likewise, has three divisions, i.e., governing, which reflects the Father, and is the role of bishops; working, which reflects the Incarnate Son who labored much for our salvation just as active individuals do for their neighbor's needs; praying, which reflects the Holy Spirit, and is the role of reflective persons.

(c) Let us now consider the Blessed Trinity manifest in the sky as in "sign " This, too, has three sections.

The first witness as "sign" is as (7) Sacred Scripture:

Then in my vision, I saw a door open in heaven.

Rev 4:1

This "opening of the door" is the witness of Sacred Scripture in which is given a triple witness of the Trinity, i.e., according to the triple law: of nature, of metaphor, and of grace; according to understanding: of authority in the patriarchs, of truth in the prophets, and of integrity in the apostles; and according to a triple interpretation: literal, symbolic, and metaphorical.

The second "sign" which evidences the Trinity in the sky is the (8) angelic hierarchy which is called "heaven" according to its threefold arrangement:

He was caught up . . . right into the third [i.e., the highest] heaven . . . and heard things which must not and cannot be put into human language.   *2 Cor 12:2, 4*

In this heaven there is a threefold witness according to the triple hierarchy, the triple order, the triple direction or performance. The hierarchy is triple, i.e., highest, middle, lowest. In each one there is a triple order and triple direction. In this way, there is a triple flowing, i.e., the highest into the middle, of the middle into the lowest, and of the lowest into the Church. This follows the triple action of cleansing, enlightening, and fulfilling. Cleansing refers to the Father; enlightening, to the Son; but fulfilling, to the Holy Spirit. This is obvious in the highest hierarchy: here there is power in judging in the Thrones who witness to the Father; fullness of wisdom in the Cherubim who witness to the Son; intensity of love in the Seraphim who witness to the Holy Spirit.

The third witness in "sign" which the sky gives to the Trinity is that (9) human nature assumed by the Word:

He gave orders to the skies above, he opened the doors of heaven, he rained down manna to feed them, he gave them the wheat of heaven.   *Ps 78:23-24*

In this sky, there is given a triple witness because Christ's is a triple nature, triple authority, triple grace. His nature was triple, i.e., physical, rational, spiritual, i.e., body, mind, Divinity. His authority was triple: kingly, priestly, and prophetic, the Holy Spirit. Grace, in Christ, was also triple: grace of headship; grace of individual sanctification; grace of transcendent intimacy. Grace of headship speaks of the Father; of individual sanctification, of the Son; of transcendent intimacy, of the Holy Spirit.

(d) Let us, fourthly, consider the witness given the Trinity in the sky in "personal mien." There is a threefold (10) eternal Wisdom, (11) Cause giving birth to everything, (12) the whole Trinity.

Eternal Wisdom is bright, peaceful, joyful:

The glory of the stars makes the beauty of the sky, a brilliant decoration to the heights of the Lord.   *Sir 43:10*

In this brightness are three reflections, i.e., the formula, expression, and report of truth. The formula of truth evidences the Father; the expression is the Son's; the report, the Holy Spirit's. It is said of the Father:

he has spoken to us through his Son.   *Heb 1:2*

Of the Son, it is said:

I came forth from the mouth of the Most High.   *Sir 24:5*

The deep was not, when I was born.   *Prov 8:24*

It is said of the Holy Spirit:

But when the Spirit of truth comes he will lead you to complete truth, since he will not be speaking as from himself but will say only what he has learned.   *Jn 16:13*

Peaceful love is also threefold, i.e., free, owed, and mixed of both. Indeed, love is "free" in the Father towards his Son and the Holy Spirit who are from him. He accepts nothing from them. Love is "owed" in the Holy Spirit towards the Father and the Son because he proceeds from both. Love is "mixed of both" in the Son who "owes" love to the Father but gives it "freely" to the Holy Spirit since the Son receives nothing from the Spirit. That love is joyful, moreover, because there is a Father who loves, a Son who is loved, and a Spirit jointly-loved.

The second witness in the sky to the Trinity in "personal mien" is (11) as Cause giving birth to everything:

He who comes from above is above all others.   *Jn 3:31*

The most powerful achievement which came down from the Cause giving birth to everything was the incarnation of Christ Jesus. In this sky witness is given the Trinity according to the threefold consideration which is most basic, most distinguished, most generous or most complete.

II. Now let us reflect upon the evidences of the Trinity given on earth. These are witnesses which stabilize our belief in the mystery of the Trinity and encourage us in the practical pursuit of virtue. That witness is given on earth, i.e., in human nature:

Thus says Yahweh: With heaven my throne and earth my footstool, what house could you build me?   *Is 66:1*

The Lord thus shows his perfection in that he directs under his commands the heavens and the angels. He also shows his authority for he touches to the "earth" of our weakness which is, as it were, his "footstool." He directs it, too, to his laws and has united it to divine nature in Christ:

and the sky gave rain and the earth gave crops.   *Jas 5:18*

On this "earth," then, the Blessed Trinity is witnessed through three witnesses: flowing water, blowing spirit, and blood. This happens through baptism which is understood by water, spirit, and blood when Scripture says, "There are

three witnesses on earth: the Spirit, the water, and the
blood.''   *1 Jn 5:7*

The baptism of flowing water gives witness to the power
of the Father; that of blowing spirit, to the integrity of the
Holy Spirit; that of blood, to the suffering of the Crucified
Son. In these three, the faithful Christian finds the practical
pursuit of virtue—first, through the baptism of water; second,
the baptism of spirit; and third, the baptism of blood. Just
as in the Trinity the person of the Father is not separated
from the Son nor from the Holy Spirit, nor is the person
of the Son separated from that of the Father and the Holy
Spirit, nor the person of the Holy Spirit from the Father and
the Son—so, neither is the baptism of blood and spirit
separate from the baptism of water; nor the baptism of
spirit separate from the baptism of water and blood; nor
from the baptism of blood is the baptism of water and spirit
separate.

In baptism of water, therefore, three things are active:
water, the Holy Spirit, and the blood of Christ Jesus:

Unless a man is re-born through water and the Spirit,
he cannot enter the kingdom of God.   *Jn 3:5*

Isidore says that ''a sacrament is that in which under a
covering of visible things the divine essence activates our
salvation in a hidden manner.''[10] The blood of Christ is
active there for from his side:

there came out blood and water.   *Jn 19:34*

Augustine comments that ''just as Eve was formed from
the side of the sleeping Adam, so from the side of the
sleeping Christ flowed the sacraments from which the Church
was formed.''[11]

In baptism there are three dimensions: that which santi-
fies; that which symbolizes; that which gives re-birth. Baptism itself gives re-birth:

It was for no reason except his own compassion that he
saved us, by means of the cleansing water of rebirth and
by renewing us with the Holy Spirit.   *Tit 3:5*

Water symbolizes; sanctifying comes from the grace of the Holy Spirit.

Moreover, the full explanation of the symbol resides in a triple expansion: in baptism there is that which symbolizes only, i.e., water which witnesses to the Father; there is that which is symbolized only, i.e., the Holy Spirit or grace which witnesses to the Holy Spirit; and there is that which both symbolizes and is symbolized, i.e., blood which witnesses to the Son who is both symbolizing and symbolized.

Likewise, the full explanation of the sanctifying is three-fold. There is that which is sanctifying only, i.e., the Holy Spirit; that which is sanctified only, i.e., water; that which is both sanctifying and sanctified, i.e., blood.

The explanation of re-birth is also threefold. There is something giving only, i.e., the Holy Spirit; something receiving only, i.e., water; something which both gives and receives, i.e., blood. Thus in the Trinity, the one "giving only" is the Father; the one "receiving only" is the Holy Spirit; but the Son both "gives" and "receives."

The baptized person, then, humbles himself under these three: water, Spirit, and blood. He thus deserves to be cleansed from sin and become worthy to enter into the kingdom of God. Because this baptism of water is the mystery of the Trinity, it is given in the name of the Trinity:

Go, therefore, make disciples of all the nations; baptize them in the name of the Father and of the Son and of the Holy Spirit. *Mt 28:19*

In the baptism of Jesus, all three were apparent:

As soon as Jesus was baptized he came up from the water, and suddenly the heavens opened and he saw the Spirit of God descending like a dove and coming down on him. And a voice spoke from heaven, "This is my Son, the Beloved; my favor rests on him." *Mt 2:16-17*

The Father is recognized in the voice; the Son is the one baptized; the Holy Spirit is seen in the dove.

Likewise, there are three in the baptism of spirit: the Spirit, water and blood. All pursuit of virtue is effected either through a way of strength, of brightness, or of love.

Strength stabilizes; brightness glows; love brings harmony. Blood relates to strength; water, to brightness; and Spirit, to love. Strength is the Father; brightness, the Son; love, the Holy Spirit.

Furthermore, spirit is triple in the manner in which it is upright and teaches us to "know." The upright spirit discerns rightly and does not allow deviations nor errors:

Renew a right spirit within my bones.   *Ps 51:12

Spirit is also holy and teaches us how to choose. In our choices is our sanctification:

Do not banish me from your presence, do not deprive me of your holy spirit.   Ps 51:11

Spirit is also guiding and teaches us to "endure" or to be active ceaselessly:

Be my savior again, renew my joy, keep my spirit ready and willing.   Ps 51:12

There are three things necessary for virtue as Aristotle states[12] "to know, to choose, to be active ceaselessly." Therefore in that one Psalm 51, the psalmist prays for that triple spirit to be given to him. This guiding spirit evidences the Father; the upright spirit, the Son; the holy spirit, the Holy Spirit. This triple spirit directs in judging lest we wander; strengthens in action lest we weaken; blesses in yearnings lest we be infected.

Water, too, is threefold. The first is that of remorse for one's own sinfulness:

It is the Lord Yahweh who speaks: I shall pour clean water over you and you will be cleansed . . . from all your defilement.   *Ezek 36:25

My eyes stream with tears because others disregard your Law.   Ps 119:136

The second is that of compassion for others' suffering and especially for those of Christ:

Who will turn my head into a fountain, and my eyes into a spring for tears, so that I may weep all day, all night, for all the dead out of the daughter of my people.   *Jer 9:1

Have I not wept for all whose life is hard, felt pity for the penniless?   *Job 30:25*

The third, prayerfulness:

Up, cry out in the nighttime, in the early hours of darkness; pour your heart out like water before Yahweh.

Lam 2:19

And you will draw water joyfully from the springs of salvation.   *Is 12:3*

Indeed, the water of remorse refers to the Father; of compassion, to the Son; of prayerfulness, to the Holy Spirit.

Likewise, blood is threefold. The first is redeeming:

Reconciling through his blood on the cross everything in heaven and on earth.   **Col 1:20*

The second is restoring:

and my blood is real drink.   *Jn 6:56*

The third is life-giving or managing:

The elephants were shown a syrup [sanguis] of grapes and mulberries to prepare them for the battle.   *1 Macc 6:34*

The "redeeming blood" is the Son's; the "restoring" is the Holy Spirit's; the "life-giving" is the Father's.

In the same way, baptism of blood is threefold, i.e., Spirit, water, and blood. Spirit is threefold: of truth, of integrity, and of final and perfect suffering. Truth is threefold: of life, of justice, of teaching. Integrity, also, is threefold: in emotions, in conversations, in activities. In perfect suffering there are three: confidence, patience, endurance. These all give witness to the Trinity. This is obvious to an intelligent person:

I am happy, Yahweh, at what you have done; at your achievements I joyfully exclaim, "Great are your achievements, Yahweh, immensely deep are your thoughts!" Stupid men are not aware of this, fools can never appreciate it.   *Ps 92:4-6*

Remember that these things are believable not only to the faithful but also to the unconverted because of the obvious seven-fold proof which is the witness to Christian faith and

to the Blessed Trinity These are: (1) infallibility of prophecy: To prophets and holy men, God revealed infallibly
many things. These things happened just as they were
foretold:

No prophecy ever came from man's initiative. When men
spoke for God, it was the Holy Spirit that moved them.
2 Pet 1:21

(2) strength of miracles: These were apparent even to
disbelievers, e.g., the Red Sea was divided; Egypt was
striken with various plagues; the sun stood still; the sun
moved backwards; the miracles of Jesus Christ which caused
even Mohammed [13] to say that "it was given to Jesus,
Son of Mary, to perform miracles." Such happenings do not
occur to confirm the unconverted in their errors!

They, going out, preached everywhere, the Lord working with them and confirming the word by the signs that
accompanied it.   *Mk 16:20*

(3) triumphs of martyrs: The martyrs' triumph is apparent
in that where one was slain, many rose up and were con-
verted to the faith. Wherever the faith of the Church was
attacked, there, especially, it grew—as at Rome. It is not
like this, however, with heretics: when they are destroyed,
others are not encouraged to follow their errors! The Lord
says:

Unless a wheat grain falls on the ground and dies, it
remains only a single grain; but if it dies, it yields a rich
harvest.   *Jn 12:24-25*

Dying heretics are not "wheat grain" but only empty
little grain-shells which only look like wheat grains. Thus
when they die there is no harvest.

(4) authority of the Councils: 328 "Fathers" were at the
Council of Nicaea which lasted for three years and glitters
with many miracles. They were men who were both learned
and holy:

But certain members of the Pharisees' party who had become believers objected, insisting that the pagans should be
circumcised and instructed to keep the Law of Moses. The

apostles and elders met to look into the matter and after the discussion had gone on a long time, Peter stood up and addressed them . . .   *Acts 15:6-7*

The Christian faith was spread abroad with much consultation and authority.

(5) renown of documents:

Immortality is found in being kin to Wisdom, pure contentment in her friendship, inexhaustible riches in what she does, intelligence in the cultivation of her society and renown in the fellowship of her conversation.   *Wis 8:18*

Truth is explained in Sacred Scripture though without definitive proof so that faith may gain its reward. However, many things are handed down to us with probability by Scripture scholars and those who have told us what they themselves had seen.

It was not any cleverly invented myths that we were repeating when we brought you the knowledge of the power and the coming of our Lord Jesus Christ; we had seen his majesty for ourselves.   *2 Pet 1:16*

We speak only about what we know, and witness only to what we have seen.   *Jn 3:11*

(6) stability of beliefs: From the beginning of the universe right up to the end, the faith of the Church endures and is not changed "even though times change," says Augustine," and what the "Fathers believed would happen, we believe has already happened." [14]

Lips that tell the truth abide firm forever, the tongue that lies lasts only for a moment.   *Prov 12:19*

God's solid foundationstone is still in position.   *2 Tim 2:19*

(7) one-ness of declaration: All the churches in all parts of the world agree in one declaration of truth and faith:

All the same, I do appeal to you, brothers, for the sake of our Lord Jesus Christ, to make up the differences between you, and instead of disagreeing among yourselves, to be united again in your belief and practice.   *1 Cor 1:10*

Let us beseech. . . .

NOTES

(1) Bonaventure, *op. cit.*, IX, pp. 351 - 357: Sermo de Trinitate. This homily is also found in the editio minor, V, pp. 238 - 249.

(2) Aristotle, *Liber de Causis*, prop. 16.

(3) Aristotle, *Metaph.* V, t. 3, c. 2.

(4) Alan de Lille, *Reg.* 4. Cf. also Augustine, *De Doct. Christ.* I, c. 5, n. 5.

(5) Augustine, *De Gen.*, lib. imperf., c. 10, n. 32. Cf. also Alan de Lille, *De Reg. Theo.*, reg. 1.

(6) Boethius, *Arithmet.* II, c. 1.

(7) Aristotle, *Physic.* I, t. 82, c. 9.

(8) Augustine, *De Nat. Boni,* c. 3.

(9) Augustine, *Enarr. in Ps.* 46, n. 10.

(10) Isidore, *Etymol.* VI, c. 19, n. 40.

(11) Augustine, *Enarr. in Ps.* 138, n. 2.

(12) Aristotle, *Ethic. Nic.* II, c. 4.

(13) Cf. Alcoranus, *Azoara* 5.

(14) Augustine, *Glossa ordinaria* in II Cor. 4, 13.

Bread

❰❰

THE BREAD THAT I SHALL GIVE IS MY FLESH FOR THE LIFE OF THE world. *Jn 6:51*

Expressed in these words is the mystery of the Sacrament, the origin of which Holy Mother, the Church, recalls today. This mystery is described in three dimensions: (1) as outward, perceptible symbol, i.e., "the bread which I shall give"; (2) as inward, imperceptible essence, i.e., "is my flesh"; (3) as beneficial and understandable result, i.e., "for the world." The visible appearance arouses the heart; the invisible existence overwhelms the mind; but the marvelous power delights the spirit.

The Scripture text, then, is "The bread which I shall give . . . " This promise was given at supper:

Now as they were eating, Jesus took some bread, and when he had said the blessing he broke it and gave it to the disciples. *Mt 26:26*

On the same night that he was betrayed, the Lord Jesus took some bread, and thanked God for it and broke it, and he said: *1 Cor 11:24*

"Take it and eat. . . . This is my body". *Mt 26:26*

Compare the multiplication of the loaves as read on the fourth Sunday of Lent (i.e. Jn. 6:1-15).

I. This Bread should be eaten with honesty and reflection:

Everyone is to recollect himself before eating this bread

Translator's Note: This is one of the homilies [1] preached by Bonaventure on Holy Thursday. He has here created a sustained image-metaphor on the theme of "bread" using the natural, understandable level as aid to touch a dimension of the super-natural, incomprehensible "Eucharist."

and drinking this cup; because a person who eats and drinks unworthily, i.e., without recognizing the Body, is eating and drinking his own condemnation.   *1 Cor 11:28-29*

Such recollection is needed because, otherwise: (a) the body rather quickly dies:

In fact that is why many of you are weak and ill and some of you have died.   *1 Cor 11:30*

(b) one will be deprived of all spiritual goods:

They all will deprive you because of the bood of a man [i.e. Christ].   *Hab 2:8*

(c) such a person becomes more and more blinded, defiled, and contaminated:

Through the street like blind men, they roamed polluted with blood [i.e. of Jesus Christ].   *Lam 4:14*

(d) they will be accused more harshly and condemmed at the final judgment: There the blood of Christ will bring charges and indictments against the unworthy:

Cover not my blood, O earth!   *Job 16:18*

Thus Christ will shout out against false priests who sell the body and blood of Christ. These are the ones who unworthily consecrate and eat. Gregory says "In the example of Judas, the Son of man is betrayed by anyone who dares to dishonor that most honored Sacrament of the Lord's body." [2] Oh! what do they do — those continual betrayers of Christ who so many times unworthily participate in the Eucharistic celebration! Oh! If many people will be harshly condemmed at judgment because of one single lack of self-restraint, singular pride, greed, or envy — with what shame will they appear who have so often betrayed Christ? Therefore, the heart of man must first be scrubbed for he is going to receive balm so precious, so noble, the whole treasury of heaven, the glory of all the angels, the Lord of all time, judge of the living and of the dead:

Anyone who eats the bread or drinks the cup of the Lord unworthily will be behaving unworthily towards the body and blood of the Lord.   *1 Cor 11:27*

Therefore,

purify yourselves, you who carry the vessels of Yahweh.
Is 52:11

II. There ought to be fervent commitment from the one
who is eating. A person would, indeed, be boorish if, when
he was scheduled to lunch elegantly with the president, he
filled his stomach with beans and lentils! Such are those who
are enraptured with wordly possessions:

You cannot take your share at the table of the Lord and
at the table of demons. *1 Cor 10:21*

This Sacrament would be desirable even if only flesh so
noble were being given as food. In reality, however, there
are three choice dishes placed on one platter, i.e., My
flesh which is tasty:

My flesh is real food. *Jn 6:55*

—spirit which is more tasty and noble than flesh:

It is the spirit that gives life. *Jn 6:55*

—divinity which is most tasty:

Blessed be Yahweh, who performs marvels of love for me!
Ps 31:21

How differently with your people! You gave them the
food of angels, from heaven untiringly sending them bread
already prepared, containing every delight, satisfying every
taste. *Wis 16:20*

Is this surprising? He is the one of whom even the angels
long to catch a glimpse. *1 Pet 1:12*

If sight of him delights so much, how much more the
taste of him? Behold the dishes at the table of Christ!
Oh unspeakable love! If he loves greatly who gives from
his own resources, how much more he who gives himself?

Christ gave himself in this sacrifice of reconciliation to
placate the Father's anger:

You . . . wanted no sacrifice or oblation *Ps 40:6*

nor were they pleasing to you, Lord, as in the Law of
Moses

Then I said, "Here I am, I am coming!"   *Ps 40:6*

Then there will be proper sacrifice to please you.   *Ps 51:19*

God, our Father, offered by Christ, your most beloved Son. Christ gave himself as the price of redemption:

Remember the ransom that was paid to free you . . . was not paid in anything corruptible, neither in silver nor gold, but in the precious blood of a lamb without spot or stain, namely Christ.   *1 Pet 1:18*

and with your blood you bought men for God.   *Rev 5:9*

seized from the devil in whose power they were. Not that the price was paid to the devil so that mankind be set free — but the price was offered to the injured majesty of God so that, indemnity paid, the devil, who had unjustly taken over mankind, could be despoiled.

Christ, also gave himself as food for our nourishment. Adam ate the food forbidden to him and his descendants unto death but Christ gave himself as the food of life unto life. But alas! for some individuals this food is not as tasty as their nature demands. Three reasons for this are: (1) infected feelings — such as amongst the sick those who, due to an infection of the throat, do not delight in food no matter how tasty it is:

Some . . . finding all food repugnant, were nearly at death's door.   *Ps 107:18*

when his whole self is revolted by food and his appetite spurns dainties . . .   *Job 33:20*

(2) over-stuffed feelings — such as in those who are satiated:

The gorged throat revolts at honey, the hungry throat finds all bitterness sweet.   *Prov 27:7*

The point is, when you hold these meetings, it is not the Lord's Supper that you are eating, since when the time comes to eat, everyone is in such a hurry to start his own supper that one person goes hungry while another is getting drunk.   *1 Cor 11:20*

Bernard comments, "Divine encouragement is of great value but is not given to those who give access to other encouragements."[3]

(3) exhausted feelings — such as in those who are weakened by hunger and so exhausted that they cannot eat:

my appetite has gone; whenever I heave a sigh, my bones stick through my skin. *Ps 102:5*

It happens in the same way for those held a long time in darkness — they cannot look at the light:

My eyes are worn out with suffering. *Ps 88:9*

Recall the story of Eli who:

could no longer see. The lamp of God had not yet gone out . . . 1 *Sam 3:2-4*

Thus one does not healthily eat the body of Christ because:

Solid food is for mature individuals with minds trained by practice to distinguish and delight in good. *Heb 5:14*

III. There ought to be genuine "thanksgiving" from those who have eaten:

The poor will receive as much as they want to eat. Those who seek Yahweh will praise him, long life to their hearts! *Ps 22:26*

because of the myriad effects of the Bread.

(1) This Bread has life-giving power: without it, no one can have life:

I am the bread of life. Anyone who eats this bread will live forever. *Jn 6:48, 51*

(2) It also has the power to eradicate sinfulness. Innocent says that "the Eucharist, if received worthily, sets one free from evil and strengthens one in good; wipes away small faults and defends against serious ones."[4]

(3) It has the power of giving glory:

He gave them the wheat of heaven, man ate the bread of angels . . . *Ps 78:25*

Similarly:

For me the reward of virtue is to see your face, and, on waking, to gaze my fill on your likeness.   *Ps 17:15*
which, somehow, is present hidden in the Eucharist.

I confer a kingdom on you, just as my Father conferred one on me: you will eat and drink at my table in my kingdom.   *Lk 22:29-30*

Woe to those who disregard this table! Not only will they not sing but they will lament most wretchedly. The servants of the Lord will rejoice but they will be dismayed:

But you who have abondoned Yahweh . . . I called and you would not answer, I spoke and you would not listen. You did what I consider evil. You chose to do what displeases me. Therefore, thus speaks the Lord Yahweh: You shall see my servants eat while you go hungry. You shall see my servants rejoice while you are put to shame. You shall hear my servants sing for joy of heart, while you will moan for sadness of heart; you will wail for distress of spirit.   *Is 65:11-14*

NOTES

(1) Bonaventure, *op. cit.*, IX, pp. 253 - 255: Feria quinta in coena Domini—sermo 3.
(2) Gregory—cf. Bede, *in Luc.* 22, 21.
(3) Bernard, *Declamat.* c. 55, n. 66.
(4) Innocent, *de Sacro Altaris Mysterio* IV, c. 44.

Twenty-Eight Marvels

〰〰〰〰〰〰〰〰〰〰〰〰〰〰〰〰〰〰〰〰〰〰〰〰〰〰〰〰〰〰

HE ALLOWS US TO COMMEMORATE HIS MARVELS. YAHWEH IS MERCIFUL
ful and tender-hearted, he provides food for those who
fear him.   *Ps 111:4-5*

The Lord has, indeed, allowed us to commemorate his
marvels in the food of the Eucharist. In this Sacrament,
28 marvels are evident: seven in transubstantiation — i.e.
the changing of the bread; seven in the continuance of the
non-essentials (accidentals); seven in the wholeness of His
Body; seven in the reality of food.

First, therefore, in transubstantiation there are seven
marvels. Bread is changed into the body of Christ yet
nothing is created, nothing broken, nothing altered, nothing
increased, nothing lessened, nothing outwardly colored, nothing destroyed.

Moreover, in the continuance of non-essentials there are
likewise seven marvels. Although the non-essentials are
present in the essence of bread, here, after transubstantiation, the non-essentials remain without that essence. Without the essence of mere bread, they continue, perform, af-
fect our senses, provide nourishment, are broken, altered,
moved from place to place.

Translator's Note: The manuscript notes "these 28 marvels Bonaventure,
at first Minister-General of the Order of Friars Minor, later on Cardinal
Bishop of Albano, a man of great prestige, knowledge, and commitment,
in a public homily at Paris preached in this manner. 'He allows us ... etc.' "
Even in this short schema of Bonaventure's homily[1] there is a succinct yet
cogent teaching on the mystery of the Eucharist. Stylistic technique, e.g.,
the careful division into four groups of seven, and spiritual teaching are
closely interrelated. At the actual occasion of the preaching, there would
be considerable amplification of each point; we have here preserved only
the "bare bones."

In the wholeness of His Body, indeed, there are also seven marvels. There is, in this Sacrament, the whole body of Christ — unbroken just as He ascended the heavens and sits at the right hand of God the Father and will come as Judge at the end of the world. Though, under the tiny sign of Sacrament and in each little part of it, He is completely contained, He is not limited to, nor formed by, its outward appearance, nor does He assume its position, take on its size, become restricted to its location, nor undergo division with it.

In the reality of food, moreover, there are also seven marvels. In this Sacrament, on Christ's own witness, his body is truly food. However, it is not perceived by human touch nor sight nor hearing nor smell nor taste. It is not experienced in the manner of food from a food-giving body nor transformed into the nature of the food-given body.

So 28 marvels are crowded together in this Sacrament. Truly, therefore,

He allows us to commemorate his marvels, since He provides food for those who fear him.

NOTE

(1) Bonaventure, *op. cit.*, IX, p. 255: in coena Domini— sermo 4.

In the Presence of Angels

〰〰〰〰〰〰〰〰〰〰〰〰〰〰〰〰〰〰〰〰〰〰〰〰〰〰〰

IN THE PRESENCE OF THE ANGELS I PLAY FOR YOU.   *Ps 138:2*

The Psalmist here indicates two ideas: (1) allegiance to the Lord — "I play for you," and (2) the method of yielding — "in the presence of the angels."

I. It must be considered that we should:

give thanks to Yahweh on the lyre, play to him on the ten-string harp.   *Ps 33:2*

The harp's ten strings are:

(1) a maintaining of reverence towards the Father, the all-powerful; (2) a watching of respect towards the Son, the Holy Spirit, the well-wisher.

He has lost these strings who said:

Father, I have sinned against heaven   *Lk 15:18*

[i.e. the Trinity], due to a lack of reverence, respect, and consideration of Divine Goodness. The remaining strings are: (4) soundness of faith; (5) assurance of hope; (6) breadth of love; (7) discernment of prudence; (8) weighing of justice; (9) sacredness of self-control; (10) steadfastness of fortitude.

It is about these qualities that the text speaks: "I will play for you on the ten-string harp." These are, to repeat, the honoring of the Blessed Trinity and the seven virtues — three theological and four cardinal. In these is found that

---

Translator's Note: This is one [1]   from a number of homilies grouped under the heading "on the angels." The homily moves swiftly and confidently to give reasonable explanations to the activities and prerogatives of the nine choirs of angels. This is an example of *"diffusius"* reporting: in actual delivery one assumes more elaboration on the various points.

allegiance to the Lord of which the theme speaks: "I play
for you."

II. The second part—"in the presence of the angels" —
indicates the method. The gloss on this text says "I look
forward to being made equal with them as now in praise
so then in merit." Remember that we should play for the
Lord by praising him in his virtues, i.e., the Angels, because of their (1) renowned high position, (2) affectionate
love, and (3) unceasing assistance.

(1) A thousand thousand waited on him, ten thousand times
ten thousand stood before him.   *Dan 7:10*

Their high position is renowned because it is close to God,
continual, open, and complete:

Their angels in heaven are continually in the presence
of my Father in heaven.   *Mt 18:10*

Thus their high position is "close at hand" because per-
ceivable; without interruption because "continually"; "open"
because "they see"; "complete" because "the face of my
Father" not however:

a dim reflection in a mirror but . . . face to face.
                                                        1 Cor 13:12

(2) There is rejoicing among the angels of God over one
repentant sinner.   *Lk 15:10*

Moreover, although they love the salvation of all mankind, they especially love those who:

work for the Lord with untiring effort and with great
earnestness of spirit. . . . Do not give up if trials come.
                                                        Rom 12:11-12

[The following texts describe]
those who "work for the Lord":

See that you never despise any of these little ones, for
I tell you that their angels in heaven are continually in the
presence of my Father in heaven. [i.e. the angels assigned
to their protection]   *Mt 18:10*

Hence also the Angel appeared to Hagar teaching the
same humility:

The angel of Yahweh said to her, "Go back to your mistress and submit to her."   *Gen 16:9*

"with untiring effort":

The Angel appeared to the shepherds who lived in the fields and watched their flocks during the night.   **Lk 2:8-9*

"great earnestness of spirit":

as the Angel appeared to the Blessed Virgin.   **Lk 1:28*

"do not give up if trials come":

But the angel of the Lord came down into the furnace beside Azariah and his companions.   *Dan 3:49*

and led Habakkuk to Daniel in the lion's den.   **Dan 14:35*

Then suddenly the angel of the Lord stood there, and the cell was filled with light.   *Acts 12:7*

(3) Consider that the angels, with their unceasing assistance, help us (a) by teaching us, (b) by defending us, and (c) by pushing us onward. This is accomplished according to the distinctions of the triple hierarchy.

In the first hierarchy, the Seraphim mould us through love, the Cherubim by the virtues of knowledge, the Thrones in the evenness of justice. The first refers principally to Religious or prayerful people; the second, to preachers or teachers; the third, to prelates and judges. The Old Testament pre-figurement of this is found in Genesis:

Jacob saw a ladder and Angels of God going up it [to gaze upon God] and coming down [to mould us].   **Gen 28:12*

In the second hierarchy, the Dominions defend us against the intensity of carnal lust that we may be in control of ourselves; the Principalities defend us against the love of worldly wealth so that we seek God first of all; the Powers defend us against the shrewdness of diabolic ingenuity lest we be beguiled by it. This is previewed:

Near my house I will take my stand like a watchman on guard against prowlers going [out to aid] and returning [to attentive considering].   **Zech 9:8*

He will put you in his angels' charge to guard you wherever you go.   *Ps 91:11*

In the third hierarchy, the Virtues push us onward to do wonders and to disregard worldly attractions:

Happy the man who is found to be blameless and does not go chasing after gold . . . since he has achieved wonders among his kind.   *Sir 31:8-9*

The Archangels push on onward to complete good deeds; the Angels, to avoid evil deeds:

Go, swift angels, to a people tottering and torn-apart, to a nation always feared, a people mighty and masterful, in a country crisscrossed with rivers.   *Is 18:2*

"tottering" through greed, "torn-apart" through envy, "feared" through anger, "mighty" through arrogance, tramped upon through bitterness, with "rivers" of indulgence. From these vices we are snatched by the help of the angels.

The angelic spirits, therefore, assist us: (a) by teaching us to acquire wisdom, (b) by defending us to gain victory, (c) by pushing us onward to gain grace, and consequently, by leading us to glory:

It happened that Lazarus died and was carried away by the angels to the bosom of Abraham.   *Lk 16:22*

NOTE

(1) Bonaventure, *op. cit.*, IX, pp. 618 - 619: de sanctis angelis - sermo 2.

The Blessed Virgin was created in such a way that she
might be utterly unmixed with the darkness of sin. . . .
The radiant-light of the Virgin, with the assurance of
grace has been made inextinguishable.'' In fact, she
even sees to it that the light of grace is not dimmed
for others. — St. Bonaventure, *Homilies*.

Light Dawns

LIGHT DAWNS FOR THE VIRTUOUS, AND JOY, FOR UPRIGHT HEARTS.

Ps 97:11

This text from the Psalms describes the birth of the Blessed Virgin as (1) noble, (2) useful, and (3) causing joy. "Noble" is shown in the words "Light." Light maintains pre-eminence in all corporal and spiritual beings. "Useful" is indicated by "for the virtuous," i.e., for the advantage of the virtuous. "Festive" or "causing joy" is seen in the words "and joy for upright hearts" because her birth should be celebrated with joy. This threefold quality, moreover, is appropriate for the Virgin whose birth we celebrate today. It is also appropriate for "light" which symbolizes her: light has "nobility" in its very visibility; "usefulness" in its abundant presence; "joy" in its bright appearance.

(1) Natural light is "noble" necause it is (a) unmixed, (b) uninjured, (c) unconfined. It is not mixed with any additional nature, nor injured by any opposing nature, nor confined by any more expansive nature.

In the same way, the Virgin Mary was, at her birth, "unmixed light" because of that grace which sanctifies. One could transfer to her, therefore, that:

"Let there be light," and there was light . . . and God divided light from darkness.   *Gen 1:3-4*

because the Blessed Virgin was created in such a way

Translator's Note: Bonaventure preached this homily [1] for the 8th of September, feast of the birth of the Blessed Virgin Mary. Throughout the homily, Bonaventure uses the image of "light" in its natural and supernatural properties to illustrate many of the special qualities and attributes of Mary and her role in salvation.

that she might be utterly unmixed with the darkness of sin. Thus to her corresponds:

She is a breath of the power of God, pure emanation of the glory of the Almighty; hence nothing impure can find a way into her. She is a reflection of the eternal light, untarnished mirror of God's active power, image of his goodness. *Wis 7:25-26*

She was "uninjured light" through that grace which strengthens:

I loved her more than health or beauty, preferred her to the light, since her radiance is inexstinguishable. **Wis 7:10*

The "radiance" of other saints, men and women, often is dimmed: therefore, it is untrustworthy to follow them lest one thinks he is following light and in reality is following darkness. But the radiant-light of the Virgin, with the assurance of grace, has been made "inexstinguishable." In fact, she even sees to it that the light of grace is not dimmed for others:

I wrought in the heavens that there might arise an unfailing light. **Sir 24:6*

Whoever follows [her] does not walk in darkness but will have the light of life. **Jn 8:12*

which never fails.

She was "unconfined light" through that superabundant grace:

And Mordecai said, "All this is God's doing. I remember the dream I had about these matters, nothing of which has failed to come true: the little spring that became a river, the light that shone, the sun, the flood of water. Esther is the river — she whom the king married and made queen . . . *Esther 10:6-7*

"Esther" in the fulness of time is the Virgin Mary in whom grace was so abundant at her birth that it can be said of her as it was of Esther:

and the king loved Esther better than any of the other women. **Esther 2:17*

It is clear, therefore, in what way the birth of the Virgin was "noble" using the image of "lights" according to its visibility with reference to the previously-mentioned triple terms.

(2) Using the image of "light," it is shown to be "useful" according to its abundant presence ordered towards a triple result: (a) to give directions to the wandering, (b) to arouse the indifferent, (c) to refresh the burdened. Light gives directions to the wandering with its sending-rays; it arouses the indifferent with its reflecting-rays; and it refreshes the burdened with its plentiful-rays.

In the same way, the Virgin Mary was "light giving directions to wandering hearts" so that, actually, in her was fulfilled Isaiah's prophecy:

The people that walked in darkness has seen a great light; on those who live in a land of deep shadow a light has shone.   *Is 9:1*

and also:

I will make you the light of the nations.   *Is 49:6*

That light began in Jerusalem but reached to the whole world:

Arise, shine out, Jerusalem, for your light has come. The glory of Yahweh is rising on you, though night still covers the earth and darkness the people.

Above you Yahweh now arises and above you his glory appears. The nations come to your light and kings to your dawning brightness.   *Is 60:1-3*

She was "light arousing listless hearts." It can be said of her:

a lamp alight and shining   *Jn 5:35*

because she not only shone to give directions to the wandering but also blazed to arouse the indifferent. Thus the setting on fire of her light was correctly depicted in Ezekiel:

something could be seen like flaming brands or torches, darting between the animals; the fire flashed light, and the lightning streaked from the fire.   *Ezek 1:13*

In her words and actions she inflamed the hearts of the Apostles and Evangelists who are meant by the words "the animals." About her, then, can be explained the text:

Flashes of lightning were coming from the throne, and the sound of peals of thunder, and in front of the throne there were seven flaming lamps burning, the seven Spirits of God. *Rev 4:5*

She was, moreover, "light refreshing humble hearts":

Light and sun came forth and the humble were raised up. *Esther 11:11*

i.e. Blessed Mary and the Lord Jesus at birth lifted up the humble, frightened, and overburdened. Mary herself proclaimed:

He has pulled down princes from their thrones and exalted the lowly. *Lk 1:52*

The lowly were invited to lay aside all earthly burdens. The poorer they were, the more they were lightened and raised up:

their intense poverty . . . overflowed in a wealth of generosity . . . *2 Cor. 8:2*

From this, it is clear that the birth of the Virgin, using the image of "light," is shown as "useful" according to its abundant presence. It is possible, however, for this light to be neutral of itself except for those who are willing to provide openness by way of obedience. Thus the words "dawns for the virtuous," i.e., that she might make them virtuous or for those who wish to be made virtuous. For others the "light" does not "dawn." Therefore, to her can be applied the text:

Though the light has come into the world, men have shown they prefer darkness to light. *Jn 3:19*

Paul says to the Ephesians:

You were darkness once, but now you are light in the Lord; be like children of light, for the effects of the light are seen in complete goodness and right living and truth. *Eph 5:8-9*

(3) Using the image of "light," Mary is shown as "causing joy" according to the reflected lustre coming from its triple quality. Light is a "cause of joy" for a person gazing upon it because of (a) its constant newness, (b) its charm, and (c) its soothing quality. For these same three reasons, the birth of the Virgin is joyful and "causing joy."

She was a cause of joy because of the newness of her exceptional privilege. Consequently it can be said of her:

For the Jews there was light and gladness, joy and honor.

Esther 8:16

because, in Bernard's words, "she seemed to have no one like herself either before her or following her."[2] Thus Jeremiah says:

For Yahweh is creating something new on earth, the woman will surround the man.   **Jer 31:22*

She, then, was excluded from that general statement:

there is nothing new under the sun   *Eccles 1:10*

because this was above the sun — i.e. through a supernatural blessing.

She was "causing joy" because of the universal attraction of beauty:

She is indeed more splendid than the sun, she outshines all the constellations; compared with light, she takes first place.   *Wis 7:29*

In the sun there is a uniform beauty but in the Virgin there is a complex beauty. "Beauty is nothing more than measured harmony" as Augustine observes.[3]

Now a great sign appeared in heaven: a woman, adorned with the sun, standing on the moon, and with twelve stars on her head for a crown.   *Rev 12:1*

Therefore she was exceptionally beautiful since:

The glory of the stars makes the beauty of the sky, a brilliant decoration to the heights of the Lord.   *Sir 43:10*

She was "a cause of joy" because of the soothing quality of her maternal gentleness. This is sweet to everyone:

Light is sweet; at sight of the sun the eyes are glad.

Eccles: 11:7

"At the sight of the sun" of Justice "the eyes are glad."
But it is "a cause of joy" and "sweet" to see and hear
the Mother of gentleness who causes joy for everyone. She
gives her children milk and honey through her Child: honey
from the taste of Divinity and milk from the taste of humanity. The Beloved says of his beloved:

Your lips, my promised one, distil wild honey. Honey and
milk are under your tongue.   *Song 4:11*

She always speaks words of peace and affection and is,
therefore, loved by all. For this reason the Church sings,
"With rejoicing. . . ."

Whoever does not rejoice, does not have an "upright
heart." Whoever has an "upright heart" reaches heaven-
ward. What great joy one should have whenever he sees
shown him the very gate of heaven!

How awe-inspiring this place is! This is nothing less than
a house of God; this is the gate of heaven!   *Gen 28:17*

May the Lord grant this to us. . . .

NOTES

(1) Bonaventure, *op. cit.*, IX, pp. 706 - 708: De Nativitate
B.V.M. - sermo 1.
(2) Bernard, *sermo* 4 *in Assumpt.* B.V.M., n. 5.
(3) Augustine, *Music.* VI, c. 13, n. 38.

"Flowers appear on our earth" since the glorified flesh of Christ has appeared in our nature. . . . In conception he bloomed because he was conceived without lust; in his passion he withered; in resurrection he bloomed again because he rose without moldering. — St. Bonaventure, *Homilies.*

Flowers

~~~~~~

MY FLESH HAS BLOOMED AGAIN. *Ps 28:7*

[Subtheme] They recognized the Lord at the breaking of bread. **Lk 24:35*

This bread is the word of God who bestows the life of grace:

Man does not live on bread alone but on every word that comes from the mouth of God. *Mt 4:4*

because:

The word of God is something alive [see that you believe] and active: [see that you hope] it cuts like any double-edged sword but more finely [so that you fear]. *Heb 4:12*

This bread the Lord has broken today. This shows that a preacher ought to modulate his voice so that he says what is harmonious and appropriate to the time and place of his homily — just as a nurse modulates her voice and tongue to harmonize with the child's. However:

little children go begging for bread; no one spares a scrap for them. *Lam 4:4*

Translator's Note: Fr. Bougerol has established that Bonaventure preached this homily [1] at the Friary in Toulouse on April 7, 1270, — on Easter Monday. It is another example of the full homily-form of sutheme and theme: in addition there is a *"collatio,"* i.e., a conference, given in the evening after Vespers. The subtheme is taken from the "Emmaus account" which traditionally was the Easter Monday Gospel passage. The theme is taken from the Psalms. Observing a twofold division of "flesh" and "flower," Bonaventure dwells at length on the image-metaphor-reality of "flower" both as it applies symbolically to Christ and also as it can be applied to each individual. Many of his statements seem aimed at current issues. There is a powerful beauty in this lyric springtime witness to Resurrection and New Life.

Some divide this bread according to rules and techniques;
only a few break it according to needs. This is that bread
by which the spirit lives when the Lord supplies grace. The
bread of the word of God must be rationed out proportionally
to the place and time and absorption-level of the congregation.
Augustine says that "the bread which nourishes mankind
kills the hawk."[2]

And so it is that I preach very reluctantly because:

It is not fair to take the children's food and throw it to
the housedogs.   *Mt 15:26*

to eat. Those things which are said rightly, sometimes are
interpreted in a distorted and destructive way. When this
bread is broken, then, indeed, the Lord is recognized. Therefore:

They recognized the Lord at the breaking of bread. This
is achieved when the mind is enlightened and the emotions
inflamed:

May the God of our Lord Jesus Christ, the Father of
glory, give you a spirit of wisdom and perception of what
is revealed, to bring you to full knowledge of him.

Eph 1:17-18

Let us, then, ask the Lord, as we begin, that this spirit
of wisdom and perception be given unto us.

My flesh has bloomed again.

According to the symbolic interpretation of this Psalm
text, the words refer to the person of Christ. According to
their contemporary interpretation, they can be said of each
and every right-seeking person. Symbolically, in these words,
the Lord discloses both the suffering connected with his
acceptance of human nature and also the joy of his divine
resurrection. The first is imaged by "flesh"; the second,
by "flower": flesh has weakness; a flower has loveliness.

Christ, therefore, says, "My flesh has bloomed again."
Flowers are firstlings; signs of a new season of growing.
They symbolize the first-beginnings of our springlike resur-
rection in Christ in the newness of glory:

Winter is past, the rains are over and gone. The flowers
appear on the earth.   *Song 2:11*

"winter,"i.e., the numbness of the fainthearted disciples frozen by some kind of icy fear. Thus Peter [chilled in mind as in body] was warming himself. *Jn 18:18*

The "winter rains" were the stormy persecutions of the Jews saying:

Take him away, take him away! . . . Crucify him! If he is the King of Israel, let him come down from the cross now. *Mt 27:42*

"Flowers appear on our earth" since the glorified flesh of Christ has appeared in our nature. The flesh of Christ was blessed repeatedly. In conception he bloomed because he was conceived without lust; in his passion he withered; in resurrection he bloomed again because he rose without moldering. He was conceived and raised in Nazareth which means "flower":

Above his head was placed the charge against him; it read: *Mt 27:37*
Jesus, the Nazarene, the king of the Jews." *Jn 19:19*

"Nazarene" is interpreted "abounding with flowers." In his conception,

a shoot springs forth from the stock of Jesse *Is 11:1*

and in his resurrection he came forth from the tomb like Aaron's branch:

On the following day Moses came to the Tent of the Testimony, and there, already sprouting, was Aaron's branch, . . . buds had opened, flowers had blossomed and almonds had already ripened. *Num 17:8*

If you believe the root inviolate since it brings forth the flower under a gentle breeze, or the flower inviolate since it brings forth its fragrance, believe the honor of the Virgin inviolate who, in the power of the Holy Spirit, brought forth the Savior. If you believe the barren branch of Aaron blossomed before the tent, believe that the real flesh of the Lord has risen and he has said, "My flesh has bloomed again."

Reflect that, to manifest the suffering connected with his acceptance of human nature, Christ said "my flesh":

He is our brother, and our own flesh   *Gen 37:27*

so that we can truly say:

This at last is bone from my bones, and flesh from my flesh!   *Gen 2:23*

Christ himself said about us what David said to his people:

You are my brothers, you are my own flesh and blood.
                                          2 Sam 19:12

For just such a relationship the beloved one yearned:

Ah, why are you not my brother, nursed at my mother's breast! Then if I met you out of doors, I could kiss you without people thinking ill of me.   *Song 8:1*

"Ah, why are you not my brother" — No bold confidence could have hoped for this if it had not been promised on such authority — and divinely accomplished! O indescribable honor manifested through the taking on of flesh by which my Lord becomes my brother!

"nursed at my mother's breast" — O fortunate those breasts which alone were suckled by the lips of the God-man, of the new-born Word! Happy those lips which alone sucked the breasts of the Virgin Mary! Happy such a mother! Happy the child of such a mother!

"my mother's" — distinguish: Mother, who may be mine and through her you may be mine since children are the possession of parents. Even though she may not be my mother, may she who brought you forth be concerned for me.

"if I met you out of doors," i.e., not shut up as previously, symbolically, in the Law but wide open, visible in our flesh:

The veil of the temple was torn in two from top to bottom.
                                          Mt 27:51

so that the Holy of Holies might be revealed.

"I could kiss you" — I kiss him in quiet prayerfulness; I kiss him warmly in active pursuit.

"without people thinking ill of me" — because of my flesh which you have taken on and in which you have accomplished for me the acts of stewardship.

You have honored it in many ways:

In our flesh you are born:

The Word was made flesh, he lived among us.   *Jn 1:14*

In our flesh you also suffered:

Think of what Christ suffered in this life, and then arm yourselves with the same resolution that he had.   *1 Pet 4:1*

In our flesh you rested in the tomb:

My body, too, will rest securely.   *Ps 16:9*

In our flesh you have risen glorious:

In other words, brothers, through the blood of Jesus we have the right to enter the sanctuary by a new way which he has opened for us, a living opening through the curtain, that is to say, his body.   *Heb 10:10-20*

So that the points we are making about this special celebration may begin to shine more clearly, consider that our flesh, because of original sin, is limited by four serious and sad weaknesses: (1) dullness, (2) ugliness, (3) heaviness, (4) feebleness.

Without any doubt the mystery of our religion is very deep indeed: He was made visible in the flesh, attested by the Spirit, seen by angels, proclaimed to the pagans, believed in by the world, taken up by the world, taken up in glory.   *1 Tim 3:16*

Bernard commented that the "sacrament of the flesh of the cross of Christ was a covering that deceived the devil."[3] Just as in the story of the water-snake and the crocodile: A water-snake who has rolled himself in mud is swallowed by a crocodile. Uninjured the snake stays in the crocodile's stomach and, when the mud has softened, destroys his devourer. When the crocodile is dead, the snake comes out alive. Thus, clothed in the mud of our flesh, the Lord entered the stomach of the devil, i.e., hell. He bit into hell because he made an opening when he freed the chosen. After he had tied up the devil as though dead, the Lord came forth and celebrated a glorious triumph. He is the "mystery made visible in the flesh" who today is "taken up in glory":

(1) Dullness clouds the understanding:

Simon, son of Jonah, you are a happy man! Because it was not flesh and blood that revealed this to you but my Father in heaven.   *Mt 16:17-18*

The dullness of the flesh thrusts the spirit downwards so that it does not understand the things of God:

Brothers, I myself was unable to speak to you as people of the Spirit! I treated you as sensual men, still infants in Christ.   *1 Cor 3:1*

(2) The ugliness is lust which is in the flesh:

self-indulgence is the opposite of the Spirit.   *Gal 5:17*

Now you, my brothers, like Isaac, are children of the promise, and as at that time the child born in the ordinary way persecuted the child born in the Spirit's way, so also now.   *Gal 4:29-30*

there is no peace for any living thing.   *Jer 12:12*

(3) Slowness and heaviness:

for a perishable body presses down the soul, and this tent of clay weighs down the teeming mind.   *Wis 9:15*

"perishable body" = debased flesh:

corrupt were the ways of all flesh on the earth.   *Gen 6:12*

(4) Feebleness:

If I may use human terms to help your natural weakness,
                                          Rom 6:19

The Spirit is willing, but the flesh is weak.   *Mt 26:41*

Christ has voided this unworthiness of our flesh by his resurrection — now, in hope — in the future, in actuality. For this reason the second theme is introduced — that of resurrection — by the consideration of a flower. A flower has four properties directly opposite to the four conditions of the flesh. A flower has (1) radiance of appearance. (2) cleanness of substance, (3) lightness of weight, and (4) soundness of stock.

(1) First, I say, a flower has radiance of appearance contrasted to the dullness of flesh. It naturally delights our sight and has grown generally to be called a flowering splendor:

a glad heart brings about a blossoming time   **Prov 17:22*

(2) In the second place, a flower has cleanness of substance contrasted to the dirtiness of flesh. Aristotle[4] says that in the basic arrangement of a plant a very light, clear fluid is distributed first into flowers, then the thicker one into fruit. Consequently, Augustine says that "a flower is purer than fruit."[5]

(3) Third, a flower has lightness of weight contrasted to the heaviness of flesh; thus it dances lightly at the slightest breath of wind.

(4) Fourth, a flower has freshness or soundness opposed to the feebleness of flesh. Thus a flower is born and nourished by the breath of a gentle wind. Thus it is that the soundness of its own original beginning is somehow or other incorporated into the flower and then in turn becomes its sweet fragrance.

The radiance of a flower symbolizes, in the flesh of Christ, the gift of splendor; cleanness, the gift of simplicity; lightness, the gift of mobility; sweetness, which arises from the essence of the flower, symbolizes the gift, in Christ, of endurance. The flesh of Christ blossomed with four flowers — rose, lily, almond-blossom, and palm. The rose is superior in beauty; the lily, in brightness; the almond, in early-blossoming; the palm, in long-blooming.

The flesh of Christ bloomed like the rose through the beauty of splendor. Just as the rose is beautiful amongst flowers, so is the splendor of light amongst colors:

like the rainbow gleaming against brilliant clouds, like roses in the days of spring, . . . so he shone forth in the temple of God.   **Sir 50:8, 7*

"Brilliant clouds" are those who have their first royal robe and await a second. Clouds subsume a clearness which follows after showers; so the saints subsume our flesh because of the desires of their own bodies.

"The rainbow," the Son of God, has a line which reflects unbent Divinity and an arc curved with the humbleness of humanity.

"roses in the days of spring" — that flesh, reddened with

blood in the springtime, which now "shines in the temple of God," i.e., the rejoicing church:

The city did not need the sun or the moon for light, since it was lit by the radiant glory of God and the Lamb was a lighted torch for it.   *Rev 21:23*

The nations come to your light and kings to your dawning brightness.   *Is 60:3*

When:

he will transfigure those wretched bodies of ours into copies of his glorious body.   *Phil 3:21*

then we will gleam like the sun whose light has been increased sevenfold:

The moonlight will be bright as sunlight and sunlight itself be seven times brighter — like the light of seven days in one — on the day Yahweh dresses the wounds of his people and heals the bruises his blows have left.   *Is 30:26*

The flesh of Christ bloomed like the lily in the cleanness of simplicity. It is said of the saints: "Your saints, Lord, will flower like the lily and like the odor of balsam they will be before you." — because of the simplicity which their glorified bodies will have when all grossness has been removed. The true nature of the flesh, however, will remain. Much more strongly is this true of the Saint of saints who due to the cleanness of his simplicity now, in his humanity, flowers like a lily. There coincides in him that perfection:

The just man shall bloom like a lily, he will flower forever before the Lord.   **Hos 14:6, Ps 92:13*

Now he climbs to the heights to:

pasture his flock among the lilies. Before the dawn wind rises, before the shadows flee.   **Song 2:16-17*

Then, indeed, the true "dawn wind rises." Then "the shadows flee" and all dullness will cease.

The ugliness of lust now causes imperfection in our flesh; the paradoxes of Scripture cause imperfection in our understanding; the obstinacy of our free-will causes imperfection in our love. But when our flesh "blooms like a lily," there will be no imperfection. There will be no inordinate desires in our flesh, no deception of our understanding, no spitefulness in our love. Oh! who does not yearn for the day when:

He pastures his beloved among the lilies. Where he rests at midday.   *Song 2:16*

Appropriately "at midday" since then is the clear knowledge of light, the full blazing of love.

He also bloomed like the almond-blossom through the gift of mobility. The almond, as the philosophers tell us,[6] because of its very fine moisture and moderate heat, is clothed with flowers ahead of all other trees. It is, then, the symbol of Christ's mobility in resurrection. When it flowers, certain smaller shrubs are also in blossom because:

Christ has in fact been raised from the dead, the first fruits of all who had fallen asleep.   *1 Cor 15:20*

and with him:

the bodies of many holy men rose from the dead   *Mt 27:52*

just like the flowers of those smaller shrubs.

The figtree is forming its first figs and the blossoming vines give out their fragrance.   *Song 2:13*

The "first figs" are both fewer and perishable while the abundant fruit follows. Few bodies of saints arose but a more abundant number or resurrections followed.

"Blossoming vines give out their fragrance" when:

they appeared to a number of people in the Holy City.   **Mt 27:53*

Yet the almond tree is in flower, the grasshopper is heavy with food, and the caper bush bears its fruit, while man goes to his everlasting home.   *Eccles 12:5*

This "almond" is Christ who has a bark of flesh, a shell of mind, a kernel of Divinity, i.e., one person in three substances. This bark knew sorrow; the shell, endurance; the kernel, joy. He blossomed in resurrection in the gift of mobility.

"The grasshopper is heavy with food" because our thin,

vagabond, poverty-stricken flesh has been filled with glory.

"The caper bush bears its fruit" — This is a perishable bush from which through mobility all need of food has been removed. It is no longer of animal nature but light and "spirit-ed."

"Man will go into his everlasting home" where there is nothing perishable, nothing limited.

He blossomed also like the palm tree in the gift of endurance which is attributed to the palm. Aristotle[7] says that "if you place a heavy weight upon the trunk of a palm tree and push and strain so heavily that you cannot endure the exertion, the palm does not fall downwards nor is it bent. It rises against the weight, presses upwards and bends itself back." Plutarch, the philosopher, advisor to Emperor Trajan, in his *Memorabilia* states that "it is pleasing, moreover, that the palm is the sign of victory in battles since this tree's nature is such that it does not yield to those who push or squash it."[8]

With the well-earned flower of endurance, Christ's flesh bloomed as he triumphed in nobility:

The virtuous flourish like palm trees and grow tall as the cedars of Lebanon.   *Ps 92:12*

Just as the firmness of cedar resists cutting into pieces, so the habitual condition of non-suffering proper to the state of glory sees to it that glorified bodies manifest in their basic qualities neither disunity nor division of parts.

By means of these four gifts, the four Evangelists declare the resurrection of Christ.

Mark shows his splendor:

Very early in the morning on the first day of the week, they went to the tomb, just as the sun was rising . . . They saw a young man [because resurrection does not know old age] seated on the right-hand side [because resurrection accepts nothing "sinister"] in a white robe [symbolizing the gift of splendor in glorified flesh].   *Mk 16:25*

But why does this description include both "very early in the morning" and "just as the sun was rising"? If it really is "very early in the morning" how can it also be "just as the sun was rising"? Peter of Ravenna[9] responds, "The celestial event reveals the truth." He had said:

When the sixth hour came there was darkness over the whole land until the ninth hour. *Mk 15:33*

The sun, therefore, which had hidden itself before its usual hour to show compassion with the Lord, went to meet the Lord with a brightness as he was rising before its usual hour. The sun in order to die together with its Creator sacrificed its own noonday brightness so that it could rise together with its Creator. When the darkness had been overcome, it burst forth before dawn. "Very early in the morning" because then the sun, to bring about "morning," came in the morning and one who had fled before nightfall, routed, now scatters the night and night must return to light those hours which terror of our Lord's suffering had seized. Gaufridus also discourses on this text from Mark. Or do we believe the sun itself visible just as it was darkened at the last moments of the dying one, so now rises more quickly in the glory of the rising Lord?

John shows his simplicity:

the doors were closed, but Jesus came in and stood among them, *Jn 20:26*

i.e., his disciples after the resurrection.

Luke evidences Christ's mobility:

And their eyes were opened and they recognized him; but he had vanished from their sight. *Lk 24:31*

Endurance is witnessed to by Matthew:

All authority in heaven and on earth has been given to me. *Mt 28:18*

What is brighter than the sun, more uncomplicated than one penetrating all things, quicker than one appearing and disappearing, and more enduring than one who has everlasting power? The elect in heaven will also have these gifts when they will blossom, i.e., those who will be citizens of that heavenly city, like:

grain everywhere in the country even on the mountain tops . . . blessed be his name forever enduring as long as the sun!   *Ps 72:16*

i.e., grass which dies in winter and grows again in summer.

This, then, is the symbolic explanation of our Psalm text.

In its contemporary interpretation, we ought to blossom on our way like the people of the Hebrews who rushed to meet Christ with flowers:

Great crowds of people spread their cloaks on the road, while others were cutting branches from the trees and spreading them in his path.   *Mt 21:8*

Joyfully does the Bridegroom enter the wedding-chamber of our hearts if he sees it strewn with flowers, i.e., with practice in good deeds. He himself is called "the Nazarene," i.e. "abounding in flowers." Therefore:

support me with flowers, restore me with apples, for I am sick with love.   **Song 2:5*

May we gain then: (1) the radiance of splendor by blossoming in wisdom, (2) the cleanness of simplicity by blossoming in self control, (3) the lightness of mobility by blossoming in justice, (4) the soundness of sweetness of endurance by blossoming in patience.

(1) We ought to blossom in wisdom to have the gift of splendor:

How beautiful you are, my Beloved, and how delightful! All blossoming is our bed. The beams of our house are of cedar, the panelling of cypress.   **Song 1:16-17*

"Beautiful" — on the inside in integrity of awareness; "delightful" — on the outside in integrity of living; "my beloved" — through openness in love to wisdom; "in our bed," moreover, is restfulness, relaxation, and enjoyment. If you wish to blossom in wisdom, may you have integrity of awareness and integrity of living. Be open to wisdom. Let your body be untroubled by vices; your heart be at peace without noxious thoughts; and your spirit joyful in its yearning for God. "Blossoming" is added: Just as bees collect the nectar of flowers which they distribute in the honeycombs and then, mixing it with a certain substance of their own spirit, they make honey, so, abandoning concerns for money, choosing the useful, let us convert whatever we select into the practice of truth.

Be careful not to choose hemlock instead of myrtle or darnel in place of wheat: "Ye lads who stoop for flowers and strawberries, Beware! a cold snake coils in yonder green" (Vergil, *Eclogues*, 3, 93; trans. by T. C. Williams). A snake is mentioned because, according to tradition, poisons are not administered except as absorbed in honey. Thus we often see, when a rose is picked, the hand of the picker is pricked by nettles. Earth nourishes health-giving shrubs as well as harmful ones and nettles often grow near roses. If, therefore, Pythagoras or Plato teach a disregard for the world, accept their teaching; if they speak of a transfer of spirits into different bodies, disregard them.

(2) We ought to blossom in self-control to have the gift of simplicity:

Listen to me, devout children, and blossom like the rose that grows on the bank of a watercourse. Give off a sweet smell like incense, flower like the lily, spread your fragrance abroad, sing a song of praise, blessing the Lord for all his works. *Sir 39:18-19*

The flower of the lily is good against inflammations; self-control against the burning of lust. Those who have been burned by fire are accustomed to seek a remedy by approaching the fire so that, whereas a stronger fire had inflicted wounds, a gentler one might cool the burn. It is a singular remedy for carnal temptations to plunge your heart into fervent thoughts on self-control. "Give off a sweet smell" that you may say:

A am like a vine putting out graceful shoots, my blossoms bear the fruit of renown and integrity. *Sir 24:23

It is said toads cannot endure the sweet smell of a flowering vine — nor can lust endure the condition of self-control. The "integrity" of "renown" will be the reward of the chaste. They will wear golden crowns:

singing a new hymn . . . they will follow the Lamb wherever he goes. *Rev 14:3-4

This is certain because — to use an appropriate image —

they did not put on their heads the garlands worn at lascivious parties, and sing with their mouths the songs of wantonness, while dancing to them with their feet. The person who, in his actions, follows the Lord, does indeed bless him. But remember that a flower is tender and delicate and often withers when touched. So, too, self-control is often spoiled when it pursues illicit contacts:

Like a vine he will let his unripe clusters fall, like an olive shed his blossom.   *Job 15:33*

(3) We ought to blossom in justice:

I am a flower of the fields, the lily of the valleys.*Song 2:1*

The "flower of the field" is justice accessible to all, shared by all, the poor as well as the wealthy. Certain magistrates and prelates are not "flowers of the field" but more actually "majesties" and "Pilates" having so many satellites around them:

with swords and clubs.   *Mt 26:55*

that they appear not as "flowers of the field" but as "well-guarded formal gardens"! Those who are so carefully guarded should be considered to have committed some heinous crime. The story is told, in the world history, that Plato said to Dionysius, the tyrant of Sicily, "What crime have you committed that you are guarded with such great diligence?"

And there are those who are neither "flowers of the field" nor "gardens." But are they "lilies of the valley"? No! They are brambles on the hillside to assail the poor! Would that those who assail the poor would recall the story in the *Attic Nights* of Aulus Gellius: Alexander the Great had subdued the farthest shore of Oceanus and had come to attack the island of Fragmaria. They sent him a letter with these words: "We have no wealth for greed of which you ought to attack us; fish-bait is ours instead of riches. In place of gold and elegance, we have cheap and rather scarce clothing. Caves are our shelter in life and our tomb in death. What place does vengenance have when there was no wrongdoing?" Alexander was moved by these words. He considered it no victory to disturb their quiet and so sent them

away in peace. Would that those who oppress the poor would
do the same!

(4) We ought to blossom in patience:

I went down to the nut orchard to see what was sprouting
in the valley, to see if the vines were budding and the
pomegranate trees in flower.   *Song 6:10-11*

You prove yourself to be this "nut orchard" if you find
sadness in the world, limitations in your body, but dedication in your heart. In a nut, the shell is bitter; the covering,
hard; the kernel, tasty. "Pomegranates" are experiences
in humility without which there can be no patience. "If
the vines are budding" — the more a flower is rubbed, the
more its fragrance is diffused. Patience grows strong in
tribulations. "Were budding" — i.e., from the past. The
bud does not come from the present. "The pomegranate
trees in flower" — i.e., those who accept the commitment
of witness. He does not say "beginning to flower" because
there are certain first-steps towards patience when virtue
is not yet completely rooted. But a person ought to be
planted in patience:

Planted in the house of Yahweh, they will flourish in the
courts of our God.   *Ps 92:13*

"In the courts of our God" — We are now on our way
in "the house of Yahweh" we will be "at home." It is
said of a certain philosopher that whenever he was insulted, he said, "You have learned to curse and I, with
conscience my witness, have learned to despise those curses."
Whenever a person is insulted, he cannot contradict all the
harmful statements. These ought to be ignored if said super-
ficially; if in rage, then show compassion; if unjustly, then
reject them. One should never become violently angry.

In these four ways we ought to blossom with beautiful
flowers. There are, however, four ugly flowers in which
we must not bloom. I will speak of these in this evening's
Conference.

* * * * *

Conference: "My flesh has bloomed again."

The subtheme text chosen was "the disciples recognized the Lord at the breaking of bread." If that bread is broken, the Lord is recognized. It is not enough, however, "to break" the bread; it must also be eaten. It should be retained in the body through frequent meditation and absorbed through constant reflection.

Those who expound upon the word of God are in multiple danger. They are in danger sometimes because those who wrongly interpret Scripture, those who poorly understand, and those who do not listen to what is said. Just as a harpist cannot touch the strings with the plectrum so that no one is annoyed by the sound, so neither can he who must expound the word speak what is pleasing to everyone — and unhappy is he who preaches to the people's wishes! Therefore, at the start, let us ask the Lord that he give me grace to preach his word.

"My flesh has bloomed again" — I have already explained that, in these words, symbolically the Lord shows us the suffering connected with his acceptance of human nature and also the joy of his resurrection. The first is imaged by "flesh"; the second, by "flower." It was also stated that in our flesh there are four weaknesses which are voided by four properties found in a flower. Through these the resurrection of Christ is symbolized. There are four properties of chosen flowers in which the flesh of Christ bloomed again in resurrection. I have also described how we ought to blossom so as to graft ourselves onto the resurrection of Christ.

But there are certain obstacles that hinder us from blossoming. We must, then, examine how we ought to blossom. We know that we should blossom because we are to be like the people of the Hebrews, i.e., going ahead so that for us, in a way, the future is already ours.

(1) We ought to blossom in wisdom through the radiance of splendor.

(2) We ought to blossom in self-control in the cleanness of simplicity.

(3) We ought to blossom in justice with the gift of mobility.

(4) We ought to blossom in patience to obtain endurance so that we can say, "my flesh has bloomed again."

(1) First, therefore, we ought to blossom in wisdom to achieve the brilliance of splendor:

Wisdom is bright and does not grow dim.   *Wis 6:12*

One who is true wisdom:

is a reflection of the eternal light, untarnished mirror of God's active power, image of his goodness.   *Wis 7:26*

Wisdom is, indeed:

more splendid than the sun, she outshines all constellations compared with light, she takes first place, for light must yield to night but over Wisdom evil can never triumph.
          Wis 7:29-30

and in this wisdom we have splendor:

Come, my beloved, let us go to the fields. We will spend the night in the villages, and in the morning we will go to the vineyards. We will see if the vines are budding, if their blossoms are opening, if the pomegranate trees are in flower.   *Song 7:11-13*

These words depict the moving of the spirit towards wisdom. The disciple, enlightened by wisdom, prays earnestly that the Holy Spirit descend into his spirit and enkindle it to such a love that all exterior things seem empty. Thus, "Come, my beloved!" The enkindled spirit cannot stand still in itself. Therefore, transcending everything, it is borne by mental "lift-off" into contemplation of its Creator. "Let us go into the fields" — the "going" is the mind's lift-off; the "field" is the mind-boggling totality of God. But since the dazzled eye cannot be fixed there except for a moment (due to the brightness of the object), it withdraws into a consideration of creatures, e.g., power, wisdom, goodness as seen in creatures. "We will spend the night in the villages" — just as the villages lead to the city, so also knowledge of creatures leads into knowledge of the Creator. The spirit experiences some dryness but, invigorated, it is imbued with new insight. By grace it rises upwards and experiences unaccustomed joys. "In the morning we will go to the vineyards" — "in the morning," i.e., filled with new insight — "we will go" because one cannot go by oneself but only with God's help. The spirit thus illuminated sees "if the vines are budding," i.e., looks at the first object, its own consciousness, and in this considers if it has an honest striving towards God. Then it tries to produce fruit from what it has learned, i.e., "we will see if their blossoms are opening." But of some it can be said:

before the vintage, their flowering is over.   *Is 18:5

Man's learning is tested in patience. "The pomegranate trees are in flower," i.e., everything is being done in the proper order. The vines grow by integrity; the flowers and fruit are produced through prayerfulness. Such a one does not seek out dissensions.

But we must take care that we are not "painted flowers": this would prevent our blossoming. The "painted flower" is the flower of hypocrisy:

The holy spirit of instruction shuns deceit, it stands aloof from reckless purposes, is taken aback when iniquity appears.
                                                              Wis 1:5

Solomon placed all the furnishings he had made in the Temple of Yahweh: the golden altar . . . the floral work, the lamps . . .   1 Kings 7:48-50

There are fakers in the "temple of Yahweh" who on the outside seem good but they:

do, in secret, things that people are ashamed even to speak of.   *Eph 5:13

To use a comparison: the painter only paints the one-dimensional exterior of his painting; so the hypocrites are "painted" on the outside and they are the ones who destroy the vineyard:

Catch the foxes for us, the little foxes that make havoc of the vineyards, for our vineyards are in flower.   Song 2:15

The "little foxes," i.e., the fakers — as Persius says:

"You will have a cunning fox still locked up in the musty

cellar of your bosom (Persius, *Satires*, 5, 117; trans. by J. Conington).

These are the ones who are a blemish on the Church. Whenever they see someone who is talented in art or some other branch of knowledge, immediately they envy him. Since they themselves are so insecure:

resentment kills the senseless, . . .   *Job 5:2*

But this sometimes creates turmoil in the community of believers. They "destroy the vines" because they are not able to attain any fame or renown in their own name and so they denounce and defame that of others. "Vines," i.e., education, perishes in many places. In the city of Paris there is more than enough turmoil in education because of those "little foxes":

Bashan and Carmel wither, the green of Lebanon fades.
                                                        Nahum 1:4

"Carmel" is interpreted "knowledge" and symbolizes good students; "wither" because many, who cannot be quiet and study, stay at home and in place of studying go hunting or fishing — and are poorly educated! the "green of Lebanon" is education because the first fruits of study are found here.

The painted flower cannot endure to be touched:

Does papyrus flourish, except in marshes? Without water, can the rushes grow? Pluck them even at their freshest; fastest of all plants they wither.   *Job 8:11-12*

Thus, of course, one sees that they cannot survive.

(2) Second, we ought to blossom in self-control to have the cleanness of simplicity:

Let the wilderness and the dry lands exult, let the wasteland rejoice and bloom, let it bring forth flowers like the jonquil, let it rejoice and sing for joy.   *Is 35:1-2*

"Let the wilderness and the dry-lands exult" — the spirit, solitary and "non-conformist" because it ignores frivolous pursuits and does not aim to please the world; "wasteland rejoices" — because it wishes to be open to God alone; "bring forth flowers like the jonquil" — these will "exult and rejoice" with unutterable joy inside and out. One who has experienced such joy cannot describe it; and one who has not experienced it cannot comprehend it. In the same way, anyone who wants to describe the sweetness of honey to another cannot do so unless by relating something about it; nor can the other know what it is until he tastes it. So, too, this joy — one who has not experienced it does not know what it is; but the one who has experienced it can only be silent. "Budding," let it bring forth flowers — in the bud is hidden the essence of the seed and this symbolizes the essence of self-control.

But there are decayed and stinking flowers which prevent us from blossoming with the flower of self-control:

Have not joy and gladness vanished from the house of our God? Seeds shrivel under their clods, the barns are broken down, the granaries lie in ruins for lack of harvest. What mourning from the beasts! The herds of cattle wander bewildered because they have no pasture.   *Joel 1:17-18*

"Come then let us enjoy what good things there are, use this creation with the zest of youth, take our fill of the dearest wines and perfumes, let not one flower of springtime pass us by, before they wither crown ourselves with roses. Let none of us forgo his part in our orgy, let us leave the sighs of our revelry everywhere! . . . . "*Wis 2:6-9*

"Wines and perfumes" refer to gourmet meals; "let us leave the signs of our revelry everywhere" — the enjoyment of pleasure is brief. In the houses of our "students," there are so many different foods and wines that they are not regarded as "clergy" but as "wine-buyers." Those fools who grow up with varied and delicate foods and potent wine appear as mindless individuals. We know that when people really become "mind-less," they are drenched with cold water; so also those who are so delicately fed unless they are drenched in strong, aged wine do not return to their senses because their digestion is so upset by these foods. (There is a lacuna in the text at this point.)

"Let not one flower of springtime pass us by" — Whatever delights us is of brief duration. Pleasure taken from foods is brief as is illustrated by the person who wanted to have a crane's neck so as to enjoy food and drink longer.

Woe to the haughty crown of Ephraim's drunkards, to the fading flower of its proud splendor overlooking the lush valley, to these prostrated by wine!   *Is 28:1*

Pompey says that gluttony stole the light of Dionysius' eyes. So, too, those who weaken their appetites with gourmet selections. As Fortunatianus states, "Gluttony bruises food and devours eyes."

(3) Third we ought to blossom in justice to have the lightness of mobility. Justice is a virtue which encircles everyone:

For you are planting plants for Adonis, you put in sprigs of foreign gods. You make them flower the same day as you plant them, as soon as it is light your seedlings blossom, but all that you pick will vanish on the day of trouble, and the evil will be incurable.   *Is 17:11*

These "sprigs" refer to useless brushwood which grows on the side of the road and is only good for firewood. We ought to blossom in justice. The sinner has planted these wild vines and sin is kindling and straw for the everlasting fire. "As soon as it is light," i.e., in the very beginning of metanoia and grace; "your seedlings bloom" — and will be multiplied by good deeds of repentance. There is deep grief and sorrow from the vision of a lost inheritance.

But those "sculpted flowers" hinder justice. There is a difference between the "painted" and the "sculpted" flower. The painted flower is one-dimensional but the sculpted flower is multi-dimensional. This symbolizes pride:

Here is the day! It has come. The sceptre has blossomed. Pride has budded forth. Violence has risen to become the scourge of wicked ones.   **Ezek 7:10-2*

"The sceptre has blossomed" through pride. The bud, i.e., the procreator, i.e., the origin of other vices, i.e., pride. If the source is cut off, the streamlets do not spread out; so, too, if the source of vices, i.e., pride, is cut off, the other vices do not spread out. Just as manure is put around the root lest the tree die, and logs are brought so the fire does not go out, so, too, whenever any substance is added to pride, it does not cease but is nourished and grows all the more. The arrogant clothe themselves with savage roughness. From obstinacy, which is akin to pride, they seek pride:

I, Nebuchadnezzar, was living at ease at home, prosperous in my palace . . . "Great Babylon! Imperial palace! Was it not built by me alone, by my own might and power to the glory of my majesty?" The boast was not out of my mouth when a voice came down from heaven: "King Nebuchadnezzar, these words are for you! Sovereignty is taken from you, you are to be driven from human society and live with the wild animals."   *Dan 4:1, 27-29*

So it is today for many people; the arrogant are not persons but wild animals. Theirs is the flower of injustice. Emperor Trajan, who was the gentlest of pagans except Titus, when his soldiers jostled him, commented, "I call the man insane who, when he has inflamed eyes, prefers to remove them rather than cure them." This shows how prelates should act towards their congregations. We observe that harpists tense their strings so that they are neither too taut nor too loose. How much more ought prelates to do this so that they are neither too severe nor too lenient. Yet it is better to be a little more lenient than to be too severe lest the string break. Those who wish to go violently through everything do not realize this. If the branch of the tree is bent too hard toward the ground by the hand of the one holding it, as soon as it is let go, it again springs back.

(4) Fourth, we ought to blossom in patience to have soundness of endurance:

Upon him will blossom my blessing.   *Ps 132:18*

But there are dried flowers. Patience is hindered through greed because the greedy are not patient:

It is right for the poor brother to be proud of his high rank, and the rich one to be thankful that he has been humbled, because riches last no longer than the flowers in the grass; the scorching sun comes up, and the grass withers, the flower falls; what looked so beautiful now disappears. It is the same with the rich man; his business goes on; he himself perishes.   *Jas 1:9-11*

"The poor brother," i.e., the pauper, will be proud. If I were alive when Christ was here in the flesh, and if I had the resources to provide him with the necessities of living, I would rather give all away and follow after him than be the one to provide for his material needs. Augustine says, "They have done well who have provided Christ, the Lord, with necessary things, but those have done better who have given away everything in order to follow' Christ unhindered." [10] Alms-giving from one's own resources is better than haphazard giving. Man's greed places a value on such things — or public opinion does. If the opinion of men were valid, tin would be as valuable as silver and gold. But these flowers are hindrances. Therefore:

"Reflect carefully . . . if vine and fig tree, pomegranate and olive still bear no fruit. From today onwards I intend to bless you."   *Hag 2:19*

So we see that we ought to blossom and what hinders us in this blossoming.

NOTES

(1) Bonaventure, *op. cit.*, IX, pp. 281 - 289: Feria secunda post Pascha cf. Bougerol, *op. cit.*, p. 176.

(2) Augustine, *de Moribus Manich.* II, c. 8, n. 12.

(3) Bernard, *Sermo fer. IV hebd. sanctae*, n. 10.

(4) Aristotle, *de plantis* II, c. 2.

(5) Augustine, *de qualitatibus florum.*

(6) Pliny, *Nat. Hist.* XVI, c. 42 and Isidore, *Etymol* XVII, c. 7, n. 23.

(7) Aristotle, *Problemata* VII.

(8) Plutarch — cf. A. Gellius, *Nect. Attic.* I, 3, c. 6.

(9) Cf. Chrysologus, *sermo* 82, n. 4.

(10) Augustine, *de bono coniugali* c. 8.

Christ, the tree of life, was filled with beauty of direction,
esteem for gentleness, visible sign of wisdom, reverence
and sanctity of life, reward of glory. — St. Bonaventure,
Homilies.

Tree of Life

〈〜〜〜〜〜〜〜〜〜〜〜〜〜〜〜〜〜〜〜〜〜〜〜〜〜〜〜〜〜〜〉

DESIRE FULFILLED IS A TREE OF LIFE. *Prov 13:12*

The coming of Christ in the flesh is described in these words in three ways: (1) totally longed for, i.e., "desire," (2) exceedingly preferable, i.e., "tree of life," and (3) manifest at this present moment, i.e., "fulfilled."

(1) Concerning the first point, reflect that Prophets longed for his coming with a fourfold reflection: (a) from reflection upon the affliction of injustice, i.e., our tendency towards evil. In this manner did David long:

Have mercy, O God, in your goodness, on me a sinner from the moment of conception. **Ps 51:1*

As a doe longs for running streams, so longs my soul for you, my God. *Ps 42:1*

(b) from reflection upon the affliction of inconstancy, i.e., our difficulty in doing good. Thus Job:

Who can grant me a hearing that the Almighty may hear my desire? **Job 31:35*

(c) from reflection upon the affliction of blindness, i.e., our incompetence in knowing truth. Thus did Tobias say:

"Can I ever be happy again? I am a blind man; I no longer see the light of heaven." *Tob 5:12*

Translator's Note: This is the schema[1] of a homily preached, again according to the chronology established by Fr. Bougerol, by Bonaventure on December 10, 1273, at Lyons in the house of the Dominicans and in the "presence of the Roman Curia." It is the second Sunday of Advent in those months of preparation before the opening of the Council at Lyons. The "tree of life" was a favored theme with Bonaventure and this brief outline offers interesting comparisons with his use of the image elsewhere in his writings.

The whole world sought audience of Solomon to hear the wisdom God had implanted in his heart.   *1 Kings 10:24*

(d) from reflection upon the affliction of imprisonment, i.e., our delay in moving towards the eternal kingdom. This is found in Daniel:

Daniel, you are a man specially chosen; listen carefully to the words that I am going to say; stand up; I have been sent to you and here I am. . .   *Dan 10:11*

There was great desire that Christ should come as justification against the affliction or injustice; steadfastness against inconstancy; light against blindness; freedom against imprisonment.

(2) Christ could not have come as a better cure for these afflictions than that he should come as "tree of life." Moreover, if we carefully consider this "tree of life," i.e., Christ enfleshed for our sake, as to (a) source, we find that it is a very special tree of life:

Yahweh caused to spring up from the soil . . . the tree of life . . . in the middle of the garden.   *Gen 2:9*

The tree of life will be for them as a scent of perfume; and they will not labor nor become weary.   *4 Esd 2:12(?)*

(b) arrangement, we find that it is a very beautiful tree of life:

On the first day you shall take choice fruits, palm branches, boughs of leafy trees, and willows from the river bank; and for seven days you shall rejoice in the presence of Yahweh, your God.   *Lev 23:40-41*

(3) fruit, we find that it is a very bountiful tree of life:

On either side of the river were the trees of life, which bear twelve crops of fruit in a year, one in each month and the leaves of which are the cure for the pagans.

Rev 22:2

(d) site, we find that it is a very visible tree of life:

the tree of life . . . in the middle of the garden   *Gen 2:9*

As an apple tree among the trees of the orchard, so is my Beloved among the young men.   *Song 2:3*

(3) Christ, that tree of life, was filled with: (a) beauty of direction:

His ways are delightful ways, his paths all lead to contentment. He is a tree of life for those who hold him fast. Those who cling to him live happy lives. **Prov 3:17-18*

(b) esteem for gentleness:

Look, your kind comes to you; he is humble, he rides on a donkey. *Mt 21:5; Zech 9:9*

(c) visible sign of wisdom:

I, the light, have come into the world, so that whoever believes in me need not stay in the dark any more. *Jn 12:46*

(d) reverence and sanctity of life:

I have come to bring fire to the earth. . . *Lk 12:49*

I have come not to abolish the Law or the Prophets but to complete them. . . *Mt 5:17*

(e) reward of glory:

Very soon, now, I shall be with you again, bringing the reward to be given to every man according to what he deserves. I am the Alpha and the Omega, the First and the Last, the Beginning and the End. *Rev 22:12-13*

NOTE

(1) Bonaventure, *op. cit.*, IX, p. 56: Dom. secunda de Adventu - sermo 9, Bougerol, *op. cit.*, p. 177.

The homilist should not be content just to preach the Word of God in the morning, but indeed, at every hour he should "proclaim his message and, welcome or unwelcome, insist upon it." The attentive person listens joyfully at any hour to words about his God and Creator.

But just as material seed yields little or nothing unless it is enriched from above with the showers that enable it to sprout and grow, so, too, unless the showers of Divine Blessings come upon these words, their yield is small.

Let us, then, ask our Lord Jesus Christ to "rain a downpour of blessings" upon each one of us. For in no one else can human longings be quieted and refreshed except in Christ Jesus. If we move away from Him, we are, indeed, empty, not fulfilled.

O God, with what great eagerness should we pursue Jesus, the one and only salvation of mankind, the totality of good for Christians, the abounding joy of the blessed! In Him wholly dwells that fulness of God-forming delight in which the spirit, immersed and absorbed, finds all ardent longings perfectly satisfied. Amen. — St. Bonaventure, *Homilies.*

Chronology of
St. Bonaventure's Life

1217	born at Bagnorea in Italy
1236 - 1242	studying at Paris
1243	entered the Order of Friars Minor
1243 - 1245	studied under Alexander of Hales at the University of Paris
1248	received degree of "Bachelor of Bible"
1250	received degree of "Bachelor of Sentences"
1252	received his Licentiate
1253 - 1257	teaching as a Master at the School of the Friars in Paris
1257 February	elected as Minister-General of O.F.M.
1257 August	recognized as "Master Cathedratus" by the Faculty of Theology at the University of Paris
1259 October	at Alverna
1265 November	refused the nomination, by Clement IV, as Archbishop of York
1273 May	created Cardinal Bishop of Albano by Gregory X
1274 May	opening of the Second Ecumenical Council at Lyons
1274 15 July	died at Lyons while the Council was still in session
1482 14 April	canonized by Sixtus IV: Bull, *Superna coelestis patria*
1588 14 March	proclaimed as the sixth Doctor of the Church, under the title of "Doctor Seraphicus," by Sixtus V in the Bull, *Triumphantis Ierusalem.*

Chronology of
St. Bonaventure's Writings

1248 - 1252	Commentary on the Gospel according to Luke
1250 - 1256	Commentary on the four books of the *Sentences* of Peter Lombard
1250 - 1252	50 *Sermones de Tempore*
1253 - 1254	Lectures on the Gospel of John
1253 - 1254	Commentary on the Gospel of John
1253 - 1254	Commentary on Ecclesiastes
1253 - 1254	Commentary on the Book of Wisdom
1253	Disputed Questions on the Knowledge of Christ
1253	Disputed Questions on the Mystery of the Trinity
1253	Disputed Questions on evangelical perfection
1253	Homily on the threefold witness of the Most Blessed Trinity
1254 - 1256	*Breviloquium*
1256	Letter discussing three questions
1253 or 1257	*De reductione omnium artium ad theologiam*
1257	Homily: *Christus unus omnium magister*
1257	First encyclical letter to the Order
1259	Explanation of the Rule of the Friars Minor
1259	Homily on the Rule of the Friars Minor
1259	Rule for Novices
1259	Why the Friars Minor should preach and also hear confessions
1259	*Soliloquium*
1259	*Itinerarium mentis in Deum*
1259	*De Triplici Via* — also called *Incendium Amoris*
1259	On perfection of life . . .

1259	Treatise concerning preparation for Mass
1259	Concerning five festivals of the Child Jesus
1260	*Constitutiones generales Narbonenses*
1260	*Lignum Vitae*
1261	Homily: the kingdom of God described through Gospel parables
1261	*Legenda Maior* on St. Francis
1261	*Legenda Minor* on St. Francis
1263	*De regimine animae*
1263	Office for the Lord's Passion
1263	Six Wings of the Seraph
1263	*Vitis Mystica*
1264	Homily: on the Sacred Body of Christ
1267	Lectures: on the Ten Commandments
1268	Lectures: on the seven gifts of the Holy Spirit
1269	*Apologia Pauperum*
1270	*de plantatione Paradisi*
1273	Lectures: *in Hexaemeron*

The following writings of Bonaventure cannot be assigned specific dates:

Determination of questions concerning the Rule of the Friars Minor

Letter: on the imitation of Christ

Letter: discussing the sandals of the Apostles

Letter: discussing 25 memorable considerations

various other official letters

1250 - 1274 Homilies - some of these have been dated by Fr. Bougerol but the vast majority are undated but span his years of active ministry.

(This chronology has been arranged from that given on pp. 182 - 183 of Fr. Bougerol's little treatise, *St. Bonaventure et la Sagesse Chretienne*.)

Selected
Bibliography

Texts:

S. Bonaventure, *Opera Omnia*, Quaracchi, 1882 - 1902, 10 volumes in folio, vol. IX Sermones de Tempore, de sanctis, de B.V.M. et de diversis, 1901. xxiv - 751 pp.

S. Bonaventura, *Opera Theologica Selecta*, editio minor, Quaracchi 1937, 5 volumes, vol. V Tria Opuscula; Sermones Theologici, 1964.

B. Aperribay, O.F.M. *et al.*, translators, *Obras de San Buenaventura*, Madrid, 1949, 6 volumes. This bilingual Latin-Spanish edition, in the series of Biblioteca de Auctores Cristianos, groups the writings of Bonaventure around a central theme for each volume. There are some "Sermones - Discourses" in volume 2 which is devoted to the "life of Christ"; there are several others in volume 4 selected as "mystical sermons."

José de Vinck, translator, *Works of St. Bonaventure*, Paterson, N.J., 1960-1966; Chicago, 1971-1973, 5 volumes: Vol. I, Mystical Opuscula; Vol. II, Breviloquium; Vol. III, Opuscula (Second Series); Vol. IV, The Defense of the Mendicants; Vol. V, Collations on the Six Days.

Life, Thought, Franciscan Background:

Bettoni, Efrem, O.F.M., *St. Bonaventure* (His Life and Thought). Trans. by Angelus Gambatese O.F.M. Notre Dame Univ. Press, 1964.

Bougerol, J Guy *et alii*, *S. Bonaventura 1274 - 1974*, Assisi, 1973, 5 volumes.

This superb publication, commemorating the 700th anniversary of Bonaventure's death, includes the fruit of recent scholarship concerning the iconography, life, work, and teaching of Bonaventure. There is also a complete bibliography.

Bougerol, J. Guy. *Introduction to the Works of Bonaventure,* translated by Jose de Vinck, Paterson, N.J.: St. Anthony Guild Press, 1963; Chicago, Ill.:Franciscan Herald Press, 1971.

This book is indispensable. The organization is excellent; it is readable and factual but deeply "Bonaventurian." It contains the only available discussion of Bonaventure as a preacher and a short analysis of mediaeval preaching. He has also established the chronology for some of Bonaventure's homilies.

Brady, Ignatius. "Bonaventure," *New Catholic Encyclopedia,* Catholic University of America, 1967, volume 2, pp 658 - 664.

This is an excellent article for the factual basis of Bonaventure's life and a succinct analysis of his significance.

Longpre, Ephrem. "Bonaventure," *Dictionnaire de Spiritualite,* Paris, 1937, volume 1, pp 1768 - 1843.

This is a beautiful article which focuses especially on the spirituality and mysticism of Bonaventure.

Gilson, Etienne. *The Philosophy of St. Bonaventure,* translated by Dom Illtyd Trethowan and F.J. Sheed, New York, 1938; SAG Press, Paterson, N.J., 1965; Franciscan Herald Press, Chicago, Ill., 1971.

Especially important in this great book are the following: Preface vii - xii; Chapter 1, "The man and the period"; Chapter 15, "The spirit of St. Bonaventure."

Majchrzak, Colman J. *A Brief History of Bonaventurianism,* Washington, D.C.: Catholic University of America Press, 1957.

This Ph. D. dissertation provides a brief, clear account. It is an excellent source for information on legislation within the branches of the Order, for papal decrees, notes on individual and bibliographic information.

Moorman, John, Bishop of Ripon. *A History of the Franciscan Order* from its origins to the year 1517, Oxford: Clarendon Press, 1968.

This is a very recent, readable, excellent history of O.F.M. There are superb bibliographies and footnote references.

Ratzinger, Joseph, *The Theology of History in St. Bonaventure*. Translated by Zachary Hayes O.F.M. Chicago, Ill.: Franciscan Herald Press, 1971.

Artistic Background:

Baldwin, Charles Sears. *Mediaeval Rhetoric and Poetic to 1400* (interpreted from representative works). New York: Macmillan, 1928.

This book is a starting point for considerations on the developments in rhetorical techniques, preaching, rhythm, and the use of *cursus*.

Caplan, Harry. *Of Eloquence:* studies in ancient and mediaeval rhetoric. Edited with introduction by Anne King and Helen North, Cornell, 1970.

This collection of previously-published-articles contains several important discussions of mediaeval preaching.

Charland, Th. M. *Artes Praedicandi:* contribution a l'histoire de la rhetorique au moyen age. Institut d'Etudes Mediaevales d'Ottawa, Publications #7, 1936.

This publication has an extensive listing of "all" manuscripts of *Artes Praedicandi* with a discussion of the various standard sections of the sermon. This is followed by the Latin texts of two "representative" works — one from Oxford and one from Paris.

Clagett, M., Post, G., Reynolds, R. *Twelfth-Century Europe and the Foundations of Modern Society.* Madison: University of Wisconsin Press, 1966.

This is the collection of papers read at a symposium held at the University of Wisconsin relative to the many creative activities arising in this important period of history.

The Metropolitan Museum of Art, *The Year 1200 — a Centennial Exhibition*, 12 February — 10 May 1970, New York: New York Graphic Society, 1970; volume 1, *The Exhibition*, ed. Konrad Hoffman, and volume 2, *A Background Survey*, ed. Florens Deuchler.

Both of these volumes are indispensable for one interested in the world in which Bonaventure lived and wrote.